Virginia County Records

New Series, Volume I

WESTMORELAND COUNTY

EDITED BY

William Armstrong Crozier

CLEARFIELD COMI

Originally Published As
Virginia County Records
New Series, Volume I
The Genealogical Association
Hasbrouck Heights, New Jersey, 1913

Reprinted
Genealogical Publishing Company
Baltimore, 1962

Genealogical Publishing Company
Baltimore, 1971

Library of Congress Catalog Card Number 67-29835
International Standard Book Number 0-8063-0474-X

Reprinted for
Clearfield Company, Inc. by
Genealogical Publishing Co., Inc.
Baltimore, Maryland
1993

Virginia County Record Publications

New Series

VOLUME I

Westmoreland County

EDITED BY THE LATE

WILLIAM ARMSTRONG CROZIER, F. R. S., F. G. S. A.

(Editor of the Virginia County Records, etc., etc.)

and published posthumously by MRS. WM. ARMSTRONG CROZIER

HASBROUCK HEIGHTS, NEW JERSEY

MDCCCCXIII

BOOK I.

TEW, JOHN, 2 June 1655; 20 July 1655.
My wife Grace Tew; my nephews John Hallowes Jnr., and Restitute Hallowes.

LOUDOUN, WILLIAM (Nuncupative), 6 May 1654; 1 October 1655.
To George Day; my sisters living in England; to Mr. Thomas Speke, gent.; to Mrs. Anne Speke.

DRAPER, JOHN, 14 January 1653; 20 June 1656.
My friend William Spence; to Anne daughter of George Watts; to John Bennett.

BOYCE, THOMAS, 1 August 1656; 15 October 1657.
To Elizabeth my now wife; to Major John Hallowes; my friend John Hillier, gent.; my friend Thomas Wilsford; my son Thomas Boyce now about 32 years of age and was born in the Isle of Wight, and in case he cannot be heard of, then to my sisters Eleanor, Anne, Dorothy and Jane Boyce equally, and my executors shall write to the Mayor of Newport and inquire after my son Thomas and my sisters whom I left in Gotyam not far from Newport, and if they cannot be heard of, then to my friends Major John Hallowes, John Hillier and Thomas Wilsford, gents.

HILLER, JOHN, 12 October 1657; 20 February 1657.
My daughter Elizabeth Rozier and my grandchild John Rozier, Jnr.; to the child of Mr. Webb my late wife's godchild; my son in law John Rozier, clerk, to be executor.

BRENT, MARY, 23 July 1657; 21 June 1658.
All my goods to my sister Mrs. Margaret Brent, and after her death to my brother Mr. Giles Brent.

BRODHURST, WALTER, 26 January 1658; 12 February 1658.
My wife Ann Brodhurst to be extx. Son Gerrard Brodhurst and in case he die without issue the land I do give him to go to my son Walter Brodhurst, and in case both my sons die without issue all the said land to go to my daughter Elizabeth Brodhurst. As long as my wife continues a widow she shall have all my land for her use and the whole stock until my said sons come of age, and if she marry I hereby constitute Mr. Thomas Gerrard, Mr. Nathaniel Pope and Mr. Robert Slye overseers of my children.

BALDRIDGE, WILLIAM, 20 March 1658; 20 July 1659.
My wife Elizabeth; my son Charles; to Daniel Hutt; to Edmund Lindsey.

MUNN, THOMAS, 24 April 1659; 20 July 1659.
Wife Elizabeth to have my plantation; my daughter Elizabeth Munn when she arrives at the age of 21 years.

PEYTON, HENRY, of Aquia, gent. 17 May 1658; 20 October 1659.
My wife Ellen; my sons Valentine and Henry when they arrive past the age of 21 years; my brother Valentine Peyton and my uncle Thomas Partington of London, draper, to be overseers. My wife Ellen to be extx.

SPEKE, THOMAS, I December 1659; 14 January 1659.
Son Thomas (under age) to be exor; my wife Frances Speke; my brother John Speke to have 2,000 acres of land if he settle in this country; my godson Thomas Gerrard; my youngest sister; my father in law Thomas Gerrard and my mother in law Susanna Gerrard; my father in law and my brother in law Mr. Robert Dye to be overseers.

MADDISON, JOHN, 10 November 1659; 10 January 1659.
My brother Thomas Perkins to be exor; my aunt Grace Isham; to John Biddle; my brother Edward Madison.

BALDRIDGE, JAMES, 26 November 1658; 10 January 1659.
To Daniel Sisson; my wife Dorothy to be extx.

ARMSLEY, JOHN, 4 September 1657; 10 January 1659.
My wife Anne; my daughter Anne Armsley until she be 16 years old or marry to remain with my wife.

POPE, NATHANIEL, 16 May 1659; 26 April 1660.
To son Thomas Pope land and plantation situated upon the cliffs, to aforesaid Thomas five cows or heifers to be given him when he shall come to the age of 21 years or day of marriage, which shall first happen. To son Nathaniel Pope the land and plantation whereon I now live; my wife Lucy Pope to have the land where I now live as long as she live or remains unmarried. To John Washington that sum of money which he oweth unto me. To my son ———; to my son in law ———; son Thomas to be exor, and in case of his death son Nathaniel.
Witnesses: John Rosier, Laurence Washington, John Washington, William Hardich.

ROZIER, JOHN, 25 February 1659; 15 December 1660.
Wife Elizabeth until my son John come of age; wife extx.

JONES, HUMPHREY, 13 December 1660; 15 November 1660.
To John Vauhan; to Rowland Evans; all estate to friend John Vauhan.

BELL, MARY, 12 September 1660; 13 February 1660.
To Elizabeth the wife of Robert Maphe; to my god-daughter Mary Maphe daughter of the aforesaid; my son Richard Bell, all estate to be divided among my children.

LUND, THOMAS, merchant; 29 January 1660; 10 February 1660.
To my kinsmen the eldest sons of my brothers William and Robert Lund; Nathaniel Jones of Machodick and James Walker of Maryland to be overseers; to Henry Paite; to my kinsman Christopher Lund.

DOYLE, CHRISTOPHER, 24 November 1660; 10 June 1662.
Teague Conners and Alexander Sumett servants to be given to Mr. Welch;

to my countryman Oliver Balie; to my countrymen Edmond Kelly and Thomas Daniel; to John Lancelott; my brother John Heabedred.

JONES, NATHANIEL, Upper Machodick, County of Northumberland, planter, 3 June 1662; 20 August 1662.
To my children; to Mary Mathe the daughter of Robert Mathe goddaughter to my wife; to Judith Eastaff daughter of Thomas Eastaff; to George Haines son of Sibley Haines now my servant; to my wife Judith Jones.

INMAN, ABRAHAM, 18 April 1662; 20 August 1662.
To Sarah Jones eldest daughter of Nathaniel Jones; to Margaret Jones daughter of the same; to Daniel White; to Anne wife of Michael Phillips; residue of my estate to Nathaniel Jones.

BROOKS, HENRY, shipwright, 21 June 1662; 3 February 1662.
My wife Joane to be extx; my daughter Dorothy Brooks; my grandchild Lidia Abbington daughter of Lawrence Abbington; to Henry Saxton my godson and his father Nicholas Saxton; my daughter Jane Higden; my daughter Lidia Abbington; Richard Cole to be overseer.

BALDRIDGE, DOROTHY, Appomatox, Westmoreland Co., 2 November 1662; 11 March 1662.
My grandson Charles Baldridge; to William son of my nephew James Baldridge; to Joshua son of Thomas Butler; to John Stands; my grandchildren Elizabeth, Anne and Mary Baynham; my son in law Thomas Butler to be exor.

MAPHE, ROBERT, 5 September 1662; 11 March 1662.
My daughter Mary; my servant Ralph Eversly; my wife Elizabeth to be extx.

PRESCOTT, EDWARD, bound to sea from New England; New London 12 September 1661; 11 March 1662.
My kinsman Henry Alldy and my friends Nathaniel Jones and Thomas Dutton to be exors. of my estate in Maryland and Virginia.

FOWKE, THOMAS, gent., 11 May 1660; 24 June 1663.
My wife Susanna; my brother Gerard Fowke to be exor.

SMITH, HERBERT, gent., 4 December 1663; 24 February 1663.
To Herbert Burwell if he lives to be of age; to Rebecca Burwell if she lives to be of age; my now wife Rebecca Smith to be extx.

CAREY, EDWARD, 9 December 1663; 24 February 1663.
To John Axton; my brother Christopher Carey.

SHORE, ARTHUR, 16 December 1663; 27 April 1664.
To Penelope Webb; my wife Susanna; my daughters Patience and Susan; my wife and George Weeden and Henry Cossum exrs.

COLE, RICHARD, Parish of Appomatox; 4 November 1663; 27 April 1664.
To the widow Brooks; to Nicholas Saxton; to my goddaughter Jane the wife of Richard Higden; to Joice Arbell; to Thomas Webb; the widow Brooks to be extx.

VAUGHAN, JOHN, 9 January 1663; 27 April 1664.
My wife Ellen Vaughan; my son Samuel Vaughan; my son William Vaughan; my son in law John Watts; my wife to be extx. and guardian of my sons.

3

REYNES, JOHN, clerk of the county of Westmoreland. No date; probated 31 August 1664.
  My servant Magdalen Jones; all the residue of my estate to John Whistens.

BALDRIDGE, JAMES, 20 April 1664; 31 August 1664.
  My wife Elizabeth; my son William to be under his mother's care during his minority.

WALKER, RICHARD, planter; 28 October 1664; 30 November 1664.
  My wife Mary to be extx; to my nephew Richard son of my brother Thomas Walker.

QUOANES, ELIZABETH, 4 November 1664; 30 November 1664.
  To my son John whose father's name is John Beard; my friend Mr. Anthony Bridges to be guardian of my son.

PEYTON, VALENTINE, gent., 27 November 1662; 29 June 1665.
  My wife Frances to be extx; son in law Thomas Speke when he comes to the age of 21 years; my father in law Thomas ———— Esq., and Mr. Robert Sligh both of Maryland to be overseers.

LANSDOWNE, NICHOLAS, 11 December 1664; 29 June 1665.
  To my wife; my daughter Mary; Colonel Valentine Peyton and John Whitstone to be overseers.

COLEMAN, WILLIAM, 12 April 1665; 6 September 1665.
  All my goods etc., to my brother Richard Coleman; my friend John Ward.

DUCKWORTH, WILLIAM, 13 July 1665; 17 November 1665.
  To Daniel Hutt and he to be exor; to William son of John Baseley.

VINCENT, HENRY, 19 February 1666; 8 March 1666.
  To my son John Lord; my wife Elizabeth Vincent; my son John Vincent; my cousin William Salter; my wife's daughter Elizabeth Ireland.

ANGIER, JOHN, 4 January 1666; 8 March 1666.
  All my estate to Mr. Anthony Bridges.

WALKER, JOHN, no date; probated 8 March 1665.
  To John Lampkin; to George Lampkin; to eldest daughter Connegan Lampkin all her mother's clothes; my son in law Henry Lampkin.

JOHNSTON, THOMAS, 14 February 1665; 10 April 1666.
  To wife Joanna; to Peter Letts eldest daughter.

MAUNDER, WILKES, gent., 20 August 1665; 6 September 1666.
  To my unborn child; my wife Sarah Maunder.

MORGAN, JOHN, joiner; no date; probated 12 February 1666.
  All my estate to William Newberry of the county of Westmoreland, carpenter.

GREY, FRANCIS, 7 June 1667; 31 July 1667.
  My wife Alice; my son Francis; my daughter Ann the wife of William Rush; to Anne Launcelott the wife of John Launcelott.

CLAY, FRANCIS, 20 March 1665-6; 31 July 1667.
  To wife Anne all my estate.

TRUSSELL, JOHN, 22 May 1667; 31 July 1667.
  To son Daniel Trussell; daughter Elizabeth Trussell, my wife to be extx.

4

WILSFORD, THOMAS, 1 September 1666; 11 September 1667.
To son Andrew Wilsford my plantation lately bought of John Watts; son James Wilsford; son Thomas Wilsford.

JOURNEW, SISLEY, 13 January 1667; probate date obliterated.
My husband Journews debts to be paid; my son Robert Jadwin; my son John Jadwin; my son Jeremiah Jadwin; to Cisely Jadwin; to Bartholomew Jadwin the son of John Jadwin when he arrives at the age of 21 years.

STURMAN, RICHARD, 5 March 1668-9; 7 April 1669.
My estate in Maryland, Virginia and England to my wife Rebecca and my three children, Richard, Valentine and Margaret Sturman; if my wife be now with child; my brother Thomas Hall and his son Thomas Hall of London, merchants, to be overseers; my friends Colonel Nicholas Spencer and Lieut. Colonel John Washington to aid my wife.

DODSON, THOMAS, 17 October 1668. Date of probate obliterated.
My wife Frances; my son Thomas who is under 21 years of age.

PAYNE, JOHN, of Cople; 9 December 1668. Probate obliterated.
Son John Payne to work for his mother until he is 21 years of age; my daughter Elizabeth; my wife Milicent; my son James.

OLATHMAN, TEAGUE, 20 December 1668; 24 February 1668.
To Walter English's children; to Thomas Collins' children; to Thomas Attwell's children.

WEBB, WILLIAM, 4 January 1669; 25 May 1670.
To son William Webb; to George Campians eldest son William; to my wife Joane.

ALDAY, HENRY, 27 April 1670; 27 July 1670.
My daughter Mary Alday; my wife Grace.

BELL, JOHN. No date. 27 July 1670.
My wife Mary Bell; my friend Thomas Webb.

WHISTON, JOHN. No date. 27 July 1670.
To son John; to Restitute Whiston; my wife Ann.

MARTIN, THOMAS, 18 February 1669; 25 May 1670.
To Mr. Thomas Pope; to Lawrence Abington; my wife; my daughter Mary.

BROWN, PHILIP. No date. 25 May 1670.
To wife Joane Brown all my estate.

WILSON, JOHN, 6 April 1671; 31 May 1671.
To Henry Dunkin and Ann Hull; to Penelope and Mary Hayden; to Henry Owen.

TUCKER, JOHN, 5 May 1671; 31 May 1671.
To my two daughters Sarah and Rose Tucker when they are 17 years old; to the child my wife now goes with; my eldest son; my wife Rose to be extx.

PHELPS, THOMAS, 16 April 1669; 31 May 1671.
To wife Ann all my estate.

BOOK II.

COLLINSWORTH, THOMAS, planter, 14 March 1690; 29 September 1691.
My two sons John and Thomas under 18 years of age; my son in law John Davis; to Thomas Greentree; my wife Jane to be extx.

STOPPER, CHRISTOPHER. No date. Probate 29 September 1691.
Robert Readman to be exor; to John and Mary Lancelott.

STURMAN, RICHARD, 2 June 1691; 29 September 1691.
Friend John Sturman; my servant Penelope Higgins; my friend Patrick Spence; friend Alexander Spence; friend Elizabeth Hardidge.

PIECROFT, NATHANIEL, 26 January 1694-5; 27 March 1695.
My son in law Edward Whetstone; my daughter Margaret; my daughter Deborah; my daughter Philadelphia; friends John Crumpton and John Tanner.

YOUELL, THOMAS, Cople Parish, 7 December 1694; 29 May 1695.
My wife Anne; my grandsons Youell English and Youell Watts and Thomas Spence; my daughter Watts; wife to be extx; to John Atwell; my daughter Winifred.

MARMADUKE, MILES, 16 May 1695; 28 August 1695.
My wife Jane; my son Christopher when 16 years of age; Jacob Remy and Morgan Williams to be trustees of my estate.

BAILEY, BASIL, 20 April 1694; 28 August 1695.
Son in law Caleb Smith; my second son in law John Smith; my daughter Ann Bailey; my daughter Mary Bailey; my wife Ann; my brother in law Thomas Robins.

SHOARES, WILLIAM, 7 October 1693; 28 August 1695.
To Elizabeth and Ruth Parker daughters of William Parker; to William son of John Landman; to Edward Minty and William Short; my father in law Mr. John Hicks.

JONES, JOHN, 4 January 1695; 25 March 1695.
Son Ashton Janes when 18 years of age; daughter Elizabeth Jones; my sons Manwaring and John Jones to live with their mother in law Mary Jones until they are 21 years of age; wife to be extx.

VEALE, MORRIS, 3 October 1695; 29 July 1696.
My three sons Morris, John and William when they are 21 years of age; three daughters Amey, Elenor and Mary; wife Dorothy; Darby Sullivant, Richard Hancock and Tobias Butler to be overseers.

SPENCER, ANNE, 29 August 1695; 27 May 1696.
Son Richard Anckram 1,100 lbs. of tobacco left to him by my former husband Richard Chapman; to Richard Chapman; to daughter Elizabeth Haley; to Ann Lucas; to two sons William and Richard Anckram; to Joshua Hudson.

EVANS, PETER, 23 November 1696; 27 January 1696.
Son Richard Evans; to Mathew Wonsbear; my wife Elizabeth and daughters Hester, Mary, Sarah and Rebecca Evans; friends Thomas Marson and Joseph Hudson to be exors.

JORDAN, JOHN, 6 February 1693; 27 January 1696.
To son Alexander Spence's daughter Dorcas; to son Patrick Spence's son Patrick; to daughter Elenor Munroe's daughter Elizabeth; to godson Jordon Weedon; son John Spence; son Thomas Spence; goddaughter Dorcas Sturman; sons John Sturman, Andrew Munroe and George Weedon; to Elizabeth Sturman; to Jane Hubard; my wife Dorcas to be extx.

RICE, JOHN, of Nomini, 26 January 1696; 24 February 1696.
Son John; grandson John Rice; son Toraballe Rice; daughter Ann Rice; son William Rice; son Ralph Rice; my daughter Elenor.

BLAGG, ABRAHAM, 4 June 1694; 31 March 1697.
Estate to wife Margaret.

MIDDLETON, ROBERT (date illegible) probate 26 May 1697.
Son John; son Benedict; to John and Nathaniel sons of Nathaniel Garland; to Daniel and Jeremiah Garland sons of Nathaniel Garland; to John, Robert, Thomas and Elizabeth Middleton the children of John Middleton, the boys when they are 21 years of age and the girl at 17 years of age, 500 lbs. of

NEWTON, JOHN, 19 August 1695; 28 July 1697.
To eldest son John my lands at Carlton and Camelsforth, in Yorkshire in England, and the house in Hull, which was my father's, also the land bought of Joseph Laycock, to said son John and his four children I leave 1,000 lbs. of tobacco each; to son Joseph and his three sons, 1,000 lbs. of tobacco each; to son Benjamin and his daughter 1,000 lbs. of tobacco each; to son Gerard Newton 1,000 acres in the freshes of Rappahannock with a mill and four negroes; to daughter Elizabeth Newton one-half of a tract of 2,150 acres and one negro; to my wife all my plate for life and then to my daughter; to son Thomas 350 acres and a mill at Totoskey; to wife Rose Newton 5,000 lbs. of tobacco and various other bequests; to son Thomas four negroes; to grandson John the son of Joseph Newton, 200 acres of land.

RUST, WILLIAM, 18 March 1696-7; 28 July 1697.
Son William; two daughters Ann and Margaret Rust; to George Eskridge; my wife Margaret.

HINES, ZACHARIAH, being bound for England, 13 March 1697; 28 July 1697.
Wife Jane; to Mary Evans the daughter of Rebecca Hurst; to Simon son of Simon Come; to Caleb Smith son of Thomas Smith decd; to William Smith orphan of Humphrey Smith; to John son of John King; William Horton to be exor.

READ, ANDREW, Parish of Cople.———
Son Coleman Read, son Andrew Read (record torn and mutilated from here on).

TASKER, JOHN, Nunc. will.
John Draper said unto Tasker, master, I pray you you are very ill and sick do you make your will. He answered there is none here at present to do it, but I will give my whole estate to you. 12 Jan. 1654. Proved by the oath of Gershon Cromwell.

JONES, HUGH. Nunc. will.
Robert Sharp aged 40, said as he was by Hugh Jones of Nominy when he made his will and gave all his estate to Walter Brodhurst, only paying 300 lbs. of tobacco to Mr. Curry, and 13 lbs. of tobacco to the deponent. John Wood aged 33 sweareth the same. 20 Nov. 1655.

BRENT, EDMUND, 26 March 1658; 20 July 1659.

Wife Rebecca; my son Edmund my two plantations; my daughter Katherine plantation at Aquia River; children under age; wife extx. and guardian. Wit. by Giles Brent.

POPE, NATHANIEL, of Appomatox, 16 May 1659; 20 April 1660.

Son Thomas when 21; son Nathaniel; my wife Lucy; my son in law John Washington; son in law William Hardidge. Wit. by John Washington, Law. Washington, John Rosier.

DADE, FRANCIS.

William Storke aged 39 swears that 1 May 1663 that Mr. Francis Dade coming out of England in the last shipping in the "Maryland," merchant whereof Capt. Miles Cook is Master, and falling sick at sea did make his verbal will in these words, that he gave his whole estate to his wife and she to have the tuition of their children until of age. Rec. 24 June 1663.

Assignment from Edward Griffith of Mulberry Island, James River, to Francis Dade son of Major Francis Dade, decd., "mentions other brothers and sisters of said Francis the heir and in case of their mortality the said land to revert to Mrs. Bethland Dade late wife of Major Francis Dade. 29 Dec. 1663.

SOLLEY, THOMAS, 12 Oct. 1663.

Wife Elizabeth my extx; my son John Rosier; my dau. Eliz. Rozier.

ASTIN, ROBERT, 28 April 1663; 24 Feb. 1663.

To Mr. Edward Nan————, all my estate.

NEWTON, JOHN, 19 Aug. 1695; 28 July 1697.

Eldest son John land at Carlton and Camelforth, Yorkshire,and and house in Hull which was my father's; the land bought of Joseph Laycock to go to son John and his four children, also 1,000 lbs. of tobacco apiece; son Joseph and his three sons, 1,000 lbs. of tobacco apiece; son Benjamin and his daughter 1,000 lbs. of tobacco each; my sons Gerrard Newton and Thomas Newton after the death of my wife; to son Joseph and his son John; my dau. Elizabeth Newton; my wife Rose.

Codicil 1 Dec. 1696. My son Gerrard Newton and his wife Rebecca.

WASHINGTON, JOHN, 22 Jan. 1697-8; 22 Feb. 1697.

To be buried near my father, mother and brothers. Wife Ann; eldest son Lawrence; son John; son Nathaniel; son Henry; my brother Capt. Lawrence Washington and my wife Ann exors; to Mrs. Eliz. Hardidge my watch which was given to me by Capt. William Hardidge's will; to my godson John Dulstone my gold signet.

WASHINGTON, LAWRENCE, gent., 11 March 1697-8; 30 March 1698.

Friends William Thompson, clerk and Mr. Samuel Thompson; godson Lawrence Butler; sister Anne Writt's children; sister Lewis; cousin John Washington, Snr., of Stafford; coz. John Washington's eldest son Lawrence my godson; godsons Law. Butler and Lewis Nicholas; my wife Mildred; my son John; son Augustine; daughter Mildred Washington; my brother Francis Wright; exors. my wife, coz. John Washington of Stafford and Mr. Saml. Thompson.

PAINE, WILLIAM, of Cople, gent., 31 Jan. 1697-8; 23 Feb. 1697.

Eldest son William when 16 years; son Edward 700 acres in Stafford; my eldest daughter Anne by a former venture; my dau. Betty; my dau. Mary; dau. Anne and son William exors; my said dau. Anne to go after my decease to Col. Lee's house; my loving wife.

CARRIER, JOHN, Cople, 10 Jan. 1697; 23 Feb. 1697.
Wife Elizabeth; father in law Joseph Hardwick.

JADWIN, JEREMIAH, 2 Dec. 1697; 23 Feb. 1697.
To cousin Jeremiah son of Bartholomew Jadwin the son of John Jadwin all my lands at the age of 21 years; exor. John Tanner; to Deborah Foxcraft; goddaughter Dorcas Spence dau. of Alex Spence; goddaughter Anne Payne dau. of William Payne; friend Wm. Bond.

BENNETT, WILLIAM, 17 Jan. 1697; 23 Feb. 1697.
To Robert Moore; to John Butler; to Sarah Tabutt; to my master Henry Rosse residue of my estate.

PAYNE, JOHN, 4 Oct. 1697; 23 Feb. 1697.
Wife Elizabeth and my children John and William.

BAILEY, STEPHEN, 8 Dec. 1697; 23 Feb. 1697.
To son John; son William; dau. Anne Smith; Anne Bailey dau. of Stephen Bailey decd.; to Mary dau. of William Walker decd.; dau. Mary Smith.

CLARKE, WILLIAM, 26 Dec. 1697; 23 Feb. 1697.
Wife Mary; sons James and William; daughters Anne, Elizabeth, Mary, Jane, and Frances.

WICKOFFE, ROBERT, 26 Jan. 1697; 30 March 1698.
Son David; my wife Margaret; my brother David Wickoff.

HARDWICK, JAMES, 7 Feb. 1697-8; 30 March 1698.
Son William land I live on; son Joseph; daughter Elizabeth Lydia Hardwick; son Joseph the silver sword and belt given me by Capt. William Hardwick; my wife's dau. Anne ——; dau. Lydia to remain with my son William until 14 years; my brother Joseph Hardwick, Henry Asbury and John Wright and Benj. Blanchflower overseers; my wife Ann.

FLEWELLING, JOHN, 15 March 1697-8; 30 March 1698.
Goddau. Margt. Flewelling; Law. Abbington exor; my two sons William and Thomas Flewelling when 16 years.

FOXHALL, JOHN, 10 Feb. 1697; 30 March 1698.
To Robert Vaulx and Sarah Elliott all my estate in Gt. Britain lying in Birmingham, Warwickshire; to James Vaulx and John Elliott; to Susannah Comocke; to Mary and Martha Elliott; my loving brother Caleb Butler exor.

CHURNELL, JOSEPH, 4 Apl. 1698; 27 April 1698.
To be buried by the side of my boy William; to Geo. Sammons; Robert Sparrow; Widow Rust; John Blyton; William Clift; Wm. Edge; to Ann Wilkeson dau. of John decd.; to Henry Pickell father of William Pickell; to Henry, John Richard and Jane children of Henry Pickell.

THORNE, GEORGE, 3 Aug. 1693; 27 April 1698.
   To wife Frances all estate.

BROWN, ORIGINAL, 5 Feb. 1697-8; 27 April 1698.
   Daughter Jane Pope; daughter Judith Roe; dau. Mary Brown at age of 16;
   son William; Law. Abbington; wife Jane extx.

TUNBRIDGE, GEORGE, 30 March 1698; 27 April 1698.
   To Mary Brown dau. of Original Brown and Jane his wife all my estate; latter
   to be extx.

NICHOLAS, LEWIS, 19 March 1697; 27 April 1698.
   All estate to wife Vasula.

PEARS, JOHN, 20 Feb. 1697-8; 27 April 1698.
   Wife Mary and my son George.

PENNELL, THOMAS, 27 March 1698; 27 April 1698.
   To Henry Hornbuckle and my godson Thomas Hornbuckle; godson Thomas
   Wheeler; to the first of my brothers' sons who shall come here for it all my
   lands.

WEST, RICHARD, 7 April 1687-8; 27 April 1698.
   To Charles son of Peter Dunkan; to John Batten; to Mary Baker; to Eliza
   Batten; Peter Dunkan exor.

OMOHUNDRE, RICHARD, 21 March 1697; 27 April 1698.
   Sons Richard and Thomas when 16; son John when of age; dau. Ann after
   my wife's death; my six children; son William; dau. Eliz. wife Ann extx.

BARTON, JOHN, 28 Feb. 1697; 27 April 1698.
   To James son of James Taylor land I live on; my wife Mary extx.

HARRIS, ARTHUR, 14 Jan. 1697; 27 April 1698.
   Wife Ellenor; son Arthur; son William all my coopers' tools; dau. Anne
   Harris; wife extx.

GORDON, ALEXANDER, 5 Oct. 1697; 27 April 1698.
   Son in law Valentine Harris; wife Elizabeth; to George son of Thomas
   Hord when 8 years old a cow yearling; son in law Valentine of age when
   18 years.

KIMBALL, LYDIA, 28 March 1698; 27 April 1698.
   Son William; son Lawrence Abington; son in law Willark Cullum; grandson
   Joseph Abington; grandson Brookes Abington; my dau. Eliz. Cullum and her
   dau. Mary Cullum; dau. Mary Rodgers; eor. Law. Abington.

MILLER, JOHN, 3 April 1698; 27 April 1698.
   To Richard Cradunck; to Philip Camose; to Eliz. Booth; to John and Wants-
   ford Arenton; to Thomas Spillman; to Eliz. Colston; to John Bell.
Inv. of estate of Lewis Delria by Eliza Delria, 27 April 1698.

WEBB, WILLIAM, 20 March 1698; 25 May 1698.
Eldest dau. Hannah Webb; my dau. Elizabeth; my coz. Ann Maiders Jnr.;
coz. Robert Mascey; coz. Ann Maider's children; to Thomas Redman; exors.
friends Robert Redman and Robert Lovell.

BEARD, THOMAS, 16 March 1697; 25 May 1698.
Eldest son John; youngest son Thomas; dau. Mary Beard; bro. in law
Robert Redman and sister in law Mary Redman exors. and to look after my
children.

HEARN, PHILIP, 18 Dec. 1697; 25 May 1698.
To Thomas Hallwell; to William House; dau. Alice Hearn; my wife Alice.

SIMMONS, LAWRENCE, 30 March 1698; 25 May 1698.
Eldest son William; son Jacob; dau. Margaret Allison; son Thomas.
Inv. of Thomas Hewes, 25 May 1698.
Inv. of Thomas Pennell, 25 May 1698.
Inv. of John Thomas by Margt. Thomas, 26 May 1698.

JOHNSTON, JAMES, 22 Jan. 1695; Codicil 29 May 1698; 29 June 1698.
Son James land in Maryland at 16 years; my four daus. Elizabeth, Barbara.
Frances and Anne; to John Gerrard my black mare; to Mary Gilbert; my wife
Elizabeth.

ETHELL, JOHN, 28 March 1698; 29 June 1698.
Son in law Thomas Shadreck; my children of age at 16; dau. Kath.; son
Abraham; exors. Charles Tyler and John Chelton.

SISSON, FRANCES BUTLER, 11 Feb. 1697-8; 23 Feb. 1697-8.
Buried near my father and mother in Appomatox; coz. Nathl. Pope; godson
Lewis Pope son of Nathaniel; coz. Lewis Nicholas; children of my friend
Law. Washington Snr. and he to be exor.

WINDZOR, ANTHONY, 7 Feb. 1697; 29 June 1698
Wife Margaret; daus. Mary, Elizabeth, Anne and Sarah.

WEBB, MICHAEL, carpenter, 12 Dec. 1697; 29 June 1698.
Eliza. Hid dau. of Thomas and Anne Hid; wife Rebecca; to Evan son of
Evan Price.
Inv. of James Talbot, 29 June 1698.
Inv. of John Payne by Eliz. Payne, 29 June 1698.
Inv. of William Clark by Mary Clarke, relict, 29 June 1698.
Inv. of Original Brown by Mrs. Jane Brown, relict, 29 June 1698.
Inv. of Geo. Tunbridge by Mrs. Jane Brown, 29 July 1698.
Inv. of John Notts by Jane the relict, 29 June 1698.
Inv. of Morgan Williams by Kath. the relict, 29 June 1698.
Inv. of Robert Wickliffe, 29 June 1698.
Inv. of John Pearce by Mary the relict, 29 June 1698.
Inv. of Philip White by Alice White alias Dunn of her decd. husband Philip W., 29
June 1698.
Inv. of John Peper by Margt. the relict, 29 June 1698.

HOGG, WILLIAM, noncupative, 29 June 1698 Recorded.
Joshua Hudson deposes that he desired Hannah Butler should have what was in his chest and the rest of estate to his brother Roger Hogg and Hannah Butler.

HARDWICK, JOSEPH, 22 June 1698; 31 Aug. 1698.
To Sarah Clark my housekeeper; Mr. Wm. Sanford Snr.; to Henrietta Buckley; to Richard Sutton; to Richard Middleton; to kinsman James Hardwick; to friend Temperance Blanchflower my bible; cozs. James and Thomas Hardwick; friend Col. William Peirce; friend Captain William Bridges; the children of William Earle to remain with my exor; friend Benjamin Blanchflower exor.

KNIGHT, TERRILL, 5 April 1698; 31 Aug. 1698.
Son Richard; wife Ellenor and the child she goes with; wife extx. and friend James Taylor to assist.

BUTLER, TOBIAS, 17 Feb. 1687; 31 Aug. 1698.
My wife and two children one not as yet in being; son James to friends John Quisenberry and his wife; wife and John Q. exors.

JONES, THOMAS, 9 May, 1698; 31 Aug. 1698.
To Frances Thorne widow a man servant named Richard Coggin having 5 years to serve; to John Mourning, cooper; to William Horton; to Thomas Longford; extx. Frances Thorne.

SMITH, ISAAC, ———p 31 August 1698.
Godson Williamson Rosier; to Bridget Rosier all movable estate and to have land in her charge until Williamson Rosier comes of age.
Inv. of George Booth by Elizabeth the relict, 31 Aug. 1698.
Inv. of Thomas Gullock, 31 Aug. 1698.

COX, VINCENT, 5 July 1698; 26 Oct. 1698.
Son Carnock Cox; my 3 daus. Martha, Ann and Eliz; son Vincent; son Thomas; sons Carnock and Vincent exors.

DAVIS, JOHN, 2 Jan. 1697-8; 26 Oct. 1698.
Son John all my carpenters' tools; son Elias; wife Ann extx.

REED, SAMUEL, 7 Oct. 1698; 26 Oct. 1698.
Son John Exor; my two grandsons David and John Peper at age of 10; son William; daus. Margaret, Elizabeth and Mary.

HARRIS, JAMES, 2 April 1698; 26 Oct. 1698.
My landlord James Coleman; friend Edward Berry to have estate.

NEWELL, JOHN, 26 April 1698; 26 Oct. 1698.
Son William at age of 18 years; friend William Horton, gent.; Mr. Richard Cradunck; my son being 10 next Sept.; exor. Wm. Horton.

MINOR, JOHN, 30 March 1698; 22 Feb. 1698.
Eldest son Nicholas; 2nd son William; youngest son John; eldest dau, Frances Minor; youngest dau. Eliz. Minor; wife Ellenor; to William Read; to Morgan Williams 20/; wife and son Nich. exors.

SULLIVANT, DARBY, 2 Dec. 1698; 29 March 1699.
Wife Elizabeth all my estate.

LENHAM, JOHN, 4 Oct. 1692; 29 March 1699.
Wife Joshan all my estate.

WICKLIFFE, HENRY, 23 Feb. 1698-9; 26 April 1699.
Mentions Mrs. Ann Washington; to Mr. Wm. Thompson Snr.; leaves his estate to a negro woman and her mulatto children and appoints Mrs. Ann Washington extx.

WATTS, JAMES, 31 June 1699; 30 Aug. 1699.
My two sons John and Spencer Watts 300 acres on the Eastern shore; wife Elizabeth extx. She was dau. of Thos. Youell (will 1695).

RUST, WILLIAM—Page is lost.

GEORGEHAM, JOHN—Page lost.

BOOK III.

Inv. of Thomas Allison by Margaret the relict, 24 Sept. 1701.
Inv. of John Purkins, 29 Oct. 1701.
Inv. of Henry Chubb, 1 Nov. 1701.
Read, Robert, nuncupative, 10 Sept. last; prob. 29 Oct. 1701.
His landlord to take all he leaves and see him buried.

BLANCHFLOWER, BENJAMIN, 1 Oct. 1694; 1 Nov. 1701.
Wife Temperance all estate and she to be extx.

VINCENT, JOSEPH, 6 June 1701; 1 Dec. 1701.
Estate to friends Erasmus Green and Richard Evans.

BUCKLEY, ABRAHAM, 23 Oct. 1701; 26 Nov. 1701.
My wife Elizabeth; son John when 21; wife and Thos. Thompson exors.

GOOD, FRANCIS, nuncupative, 26 Nov. 1701; 1 Dec. 1701.
Estate to friends in Ireland if anything left after burial.

SCOTT, JOHN, of Mattex, 28 May 1700; 2 Dec. 1701.
My two sisters and their children that I believe are in Ireland and whose maiden names are Jane and Rebecca Scott £100; my bro. James' son named Gustavus; my bro. Gustavus; to son John land I now dwell on; my dau. Jane; my wife Sarah; son John when 8 or 9 to go to England to my brother Gustavus of Bristol to be educated; exors. William Graham and Andrew Munroe; mentions wife's former husband Mr. George Cross and their child George Cross.
Inv. of Thomas White, 1 Dec. 1701.
Inv. of Walter English late of Par. of Cople 1 Dec. 1701.
Inv. of Mr. John Clements by Jane C. the admx. 28 Jan. 1701.

BUCKLEY, ABRAHAM, nuncupative, 28 Jan. 1701; 2 Feb. 1701.
Elizabeth the relict to guardian to son John.

ROBERTS, MAURICE, nuncupative, 17 Dec. 1701; 2 Feb. 1701.
All estate to John Igdon.

PIERCE, COLONEL WILLIAM, of Cople, gent.; 20 Feb. 1701; 7 April 1702.
To Pierce and Stanley Gower 300 acres of land; grandson Samuel Bayley; Grandson William Pierce at 20 years of age; daus. Elizabeth Bridges, Margaret Graham and Mary Rowsey; to Thomas Marson and Rachel his wife; exors. Thomas Marson and grandson Wm. Pierce; my son John Pierce the decd. father of grandson William my wife.

TILSON, ROGER, 24 Oct. 1701; 29 April 1702.
Daughter Rebecca when 18; son Robert when 17; wife Hannah; exor. William Carr and George Eskridge.
(NOTE. Body of will calls testator Robert but sig. is Roger.)
Inv. of William Lambee, 9 April 1702.
Inv. of Luke Demenet by Mary Cockerill the relict, 29 April 1702.
App. of estate of Edward Paine, 8 June 1702.
Supp. inv. of Capt. John Scott, 1 Sept. 1702.

WILLIAMS, JOHN, planter, 27 May 1702; 26 Aug. 1702.
Son John; dau. Susan Jones; dau. Ann Tillary; dau. Jane Walker; dau. Elizabeth; dau. Mary Laham; grandau. Elizabeth Walker; wife Jane.
Inv. of John Hawkins, merchant, 25 Aug. 1702.
Inv. of Robert Smith by Robt. Johnson and Mary his wife, 1 Sept. 1702.

DUDLEY, RICHARD, 27 Oct. 1702, 25 Nov. 1702.
To John Cockerill land by West. Court House; to John Follings; to James Taylor's son William; wife Mary Dudley extx.

BOOTH, WILLIAM, 2 Oct. 1702; 25 Nov. 1702.
Wife Elizabeth; to Mary Abingdon dau. of Law. A.; to Alex. Webster and Ann his wife; to Sarah wife of Capt. Benj. Berryman; to Thomas Shaw; sister in law Sarah wife of John Blagdon late of this co. decd., to be extx.

HALEY, EDWARD, 5 Nov. 1702; 2 Dec. 1702.
Wife Sarah; son John a year old 19 Dec. 1702; daughter Elizabeth 4 years old 11 of Aug. 1703.
Inv. of John Rozier, 25 Nov. 1702.

CAMPBELL, JAMES, 20 Nov. 1702; 30 Dec. 1702.
To John Higdon's three sons, Original, Daniel and John when 20; to Nathl. Pope's two children, Mary and William late of Richmond co., when 21 years; to Elizabeth Higgins' two sons; to Mary Triplett; to Original Roe; wife Jane extx.

ALLERTON, ISAAC, 25 Oct. 1702; 30 Dec. 1702.
Daughter Sarah Lee and grandson Allerton Newton land in Stafford; dau. Elizabeth Starr who lives in New England; my dau. Travers and her three daughters Elizabeth, Rebecca and Winifred Travers; son Willoughby Allerton exor.
Inv. of John Canada, 30 Dec. 1702.

CARR, WILLIAM, 13 Jan. 1702-3; 24 Feb. 1703.
Son Joseph; daughters Sarah, Elizabeth, Hannah, Martha, Mary, Ann and Jane Carr; wife Sarah; grandsons Daniel McCarty and Geo. Eskridge.

FOSTER, ROBERT, 8 Oct. 1702; 24 Feb. 1702.
Godson Robert Marcy; goddau. Sarah Beard; goddau. Mary Walker; godson William Graham; wife Ann extx.

BENNETT, WILLIAM, 2 Feb. 1702-3; 24 Feb. 1703.
Son Corscomb; dau. Margaret plantat. in Stafford; my wife and her son Christopher; my two sons in law John and Thomas Christopher; friend Daniel Field trustee.

JONES, STEPHEN, gent.; Cople, 30 Jan. 1702-3; 31 March 1703.
To Lettice wife of the Honl. Richard Lee; to Robert Osborne for making my will; to Paul Howell.

GARLAND, NATHANIEL, 16 Jan. 1702; 31 March 1703.
Whereas Robert Middleton and Mary his wife did in their lifetime give to my sons John and Nathaniel each a mare and whereas both sons are dead, etc., my son Jeremiah Garland exor; my brother Thomas Garland to be guard. until son is 21.

Inv. of Geo. Sheppard by Eliz. Sheppard alias Thornbury, 31 Mch. 1703.

BONAM, SAMUEL, 14 Feb. 1702; 5 May 1703.
My three sons Samuel, Philpot and Daniel; wife Katherine extx.

Inv. of Henry Pickerill by Elizabeth P. 5 May 1703.
Inv. of Jacob Lucas by Charles Lucas, 5 May 1703.

ATWELL, CAPT. THOMAS, gent., 13 March 1702-3; 26 May 1703.
Brothers Francis and John Atwell; son Francis; to Thomas son of my bro. John Atwell; to Ann Pye dau. of John Pye, decd.; Frances and Hannah Tanner daus. of Thomas and Mary Tanner; bro. Francis exor.

WEBSTER, ALEXANDER, 2 May 1688; 26 May 1703.
Wife Ann extx.

GARNER, JOHN, 22 Jan. 1702; 1 Jan. 1703.
Sons John, Henry, Vincent, Parish, Benjamin and James; daus. Mary Susan (Note no comma, so may be either Mary or Mary Susan) dau. Martha; wife Susan.

Inv. of Paul Horrell, by Elizabeth Horrell, 6 July 1703.
Inv. of Benj. Henman, 6 July 1703.

ROBINS, SIMON, 28 June 1703; 25 Aug. 1703.
To Ellis Brown; my servant Owen Brannan; to Sarah Newstubbs; to Simon Lyn; to James Brown and Robert Phillips.

WOODLOCK, THOMAS, 10 Feb 1702-3; 25 Aug. 1703.
Estate to Ruth Coneland, widow.

ORCHARD, JAMES, 24 April 1694; 29 Sept. 1703.
Estate to wife Rebecca.

15

SCOTT, JANE, Inv. of est. most being that of her decd. father Mr. John Scott, Sept. 1703.
Inv. of David Thomas by Mary Thomas, 1 Dec. 1703.

LEGG, ROBERT, 12 Feb. 1702-3; 1 Dec. 1703.
Wife Mary to have care of son James till 18 and dau. Eliz. till 16.
Inv. of Randle Davenport by Mary Davenport, 1 Dec. 1703.

WILSFORD, THOMAS, gent., 17 Sept. 1700; 23 Feb. 1703.
Friend Richard Watts all my land.

KNOBLE, ROBERT, medicus, 25 Feb. 1703-4; 23 Feb. 1704.
To friend Lewis Markham all goods in Va. for the use of my wife Mary and my three youngest children and he to be exor.

WARE, JOHN, 24 July 1703; 29 March 1704.
Son John; dau. Elizabeth Ware; sons in law Anthony Morgan and Robert Morgan; wife Elizabeth extx.

REDMAN, ROBERT, 18 Jan. 1703; 29 March 1704.
To Thos. Beord; to Mary Lovel; my son Francis exor.

ROZIER, BRIDGES, 29 Jan. 1703; 29 March 1704.
Son John; my wife Elizabeth extx.

WEEDON, GEORGE, 5 Sept. 1703; 29 March 1704.
Son Jordan; dau. Mary Weedon; to George son of Thomas Weedon and George son of Benjamin Weedon; wife Susannah; brother John Weedon son Jordan and wife exors; overseers Andrew Munroe, John Washington and Thomas Weedon.

MARSHALL, THOMAS, carpenter, ———; 31 May 1704.
Wife Martha extx. and if she should marry then John Brown, Snr. and John Brown Jnr. to be guardians to my children; to Eliz. Rozier; son William my plantation when of age.
Inv. of Edward Hull, 31 May 1704.
Inv. of Francis Randolph by Henrietta Randolph, 31 May 1704.

HUDSON, JOSHUA, 6 June 1704; 26 July 1704.
Son John plantation he now lives on; son Joshua 100 acres; sons Caleb and Rush Hudson; wife Eliz. extx.

WICKERS, THOMAS, 4 April 1704; 26 July 1704.
Son Benjamin; to George Cross my exors.; son in law; to Thomas Chancellor; to Charles Tankersley; Jacob Martyn exor.
Inv. of Robert Nobell, 26 July 1704.

SPENCE, ALEXANDER, gent., of Yocomico, 2 May 1704; 30 Aug. 1704.
Son Patrick; dau. Mary Spence; daus. Dorcas and Eliz. Spence; to my wife I bequeath nothing but her wearing apparel; friends Wm. Allerton and Geo. Eskridge exors.
Inv. of John Ware by Eliz. Ware, 27 Sept. 1704.
Deed of gift from Chap. Dark to Sarah, Ann, Eliz. and Margt. Hudson, daus. of Joshua Hudson lately decd., 31 Jan. 1704.
Inv. of George Thorne Jr. by Frances Thorne, 28 Feb. 1704.

HARDWICK, GEORGE, planter, 27 May 1704; 28 Feb. 1704.
To son Robert and his son George when latter is 18; my wife Mary; to Mary, Kath and Susannah Stewart daus. of Wm. Stewart; to Blanche Hopkins dau. of Rice Hopkins; exor. James Westcomb.

ROZIER, JOHN, 28 Sept. 1705; 31 Oct. 1705.
To Nathl. Pope clerk of Stafford all land which I formerly gave to my dau. Elizabeth Leftwich; rest to wife Mary Rozier.

Inv. of Erasmus Green, 27 Feb. 1705.
Inv. of Mrs. Martha Flint, 5 March 1705.
Inv. of Richard Jarvis, 4 April 1706.

WELLINGTON, MICHAEL, 9 Oct. 1701; 27 March 1706.
Dau. Ann Robinson; grandson Wm. Robinson; grandson Michael Robinson; granddau. Elizabeth Blundell; my wife and my son John my house and good will in Coadrill (?) Co. of Hereford, Gt. Britain.

Inv. of William Lancelott, 26 June 1706; by Jane the relict.
Inv. of Henry Wharton by Eliz. Wharton, 26 June 1706.

CARTER, FRANCES, wife of Thomas Carter, decd. of West. 22 July 1706; 28 Aug. 1706.
Joseph Hennings and Thomas Butler exors; Daniel Mills and Thomas Langford; to Gerard Ford; estate to my exors.

MIDDLETON, JOHN, 14 March 1705-6; 25 Sept. 1706.
Sons John, Robert and Benjamin; daus. Elizabeth, Mary and Alice Middleton; son Thomas; wife Elizabeth; sons all under 21; son John exor; my brother Benedict Middleton and William Hammock exors.

BOOK IV.
Inv. of John Rice by Eliz. Rice, 22 Feb. 1706.
HORNBUCKLE, HENRY, 11 Oct. 1704; 26 March 1707.
Wife Ellenor; sons Thomas and Richard.

BEARD, ANTHONY, 23 Oct. ———; 26 March 1707.
Sons John and Andrew; dau. Sarah; wife Elizabeth.

ASBURY, HENRY, 3 Feb. 1706; 30 April 1707.
Sons Henry, Thomas and Benjamin; dau. Catherine; wife Mary extx.

BROWN, THOMAS, 14 March 1706; 30 April 1707.
Wife Elizabeth; dau. Frances Brown; sons George and Thomas; my brothers George and William Brown.

SMOOT, WILLIAM, 12 April 1706; 30 April 1707.
Daughters Sarah and Mary Smoot; wife Ellenor; sons Wm. and Thomas.

Inv. of John Piper, mentions that Thos. Harper had married the relic of J. Piper. Rec. 25 June 1707.
Inv. of Roger Hogg, 24 Sept. 1707.

SMITH, WILLIAM, 10 Oct. 1707; 26 Nov. 1707.
My wife; granddaus. Jane and Sarah Ashton; dau. Temperance Lucas; dau. Mary King; son in law William Danks; grandson Smith King; wife, daus. Temp. and Mary exors.

17

COLE, ROBERT, 7 Feb. 1707; 25 Feb. 1707.
Son Marydoz Cole; wife Mary extx.

UNDERWOOD, MARY, 9 Jan. 1707-8; 25 Feb. 1707.
All estate to Morris Hurley.
Inv. of William Cohoren, 25 Feb. 1707.
Inv. of Roger Moss by Eliz. Moss, 25 Feb. 1707.

ELLIOTT, JOHN, 9 Jan. 1707; 31 March 1708.
Sons John and William; wife Sara extx.
Inv. of John Manner, 4 April 1708.
Inv. of William Saxton 31 March 1708.
Inv. of William Powell 31 March 1708.
Inv. of Richard Hancock, 31 March 1708.

CHILTON, JOHN, Snr., 15 Nov. 1706; 29 April 1708.
Daughter Sarah Chilton; dau. Mary wife of John Sharp of Lancaster; dau Elizabeth wife of Bryan Groves; son Thomas; grandson John son of William Chilton; grandson John son of John Chilton; wife Jane and all my children; son John exor.

HUDSON, JOHN, 22 April 1708; 28 July 1708.
Dau. Margaret plantation I live on; dau. Mary plant. where Edwd. Manning lives; uncle William Rush and brother Joshua Hudson exors; daus. of age at 16.

SPENCER, JOHN, of Nominy, gent.; 20 June 1708; 28 Aug. 1708.
To Joseph Taylor, planter; son Nicholas Spencer; dau. Frances Spencer; wife Mary extx.

CASH, WILLIAM, 16 Feb. 1707; 25 Aug. 1708.
Wife Elizabeth extx; sons William, Thomas, John, James, Howard and Peter; William 19 years old 5 March 1708; Thomas 11 years old 2 Aug. 1708; Anish Cash 15 years old 31 July 1708.

TANNER, THOMAS, 10 Aug. 1708; 29 Sept. 1708.
Sister Hannah Tanner of Honiton in Devon if living; daus. Frances and Hannah Tanner.

JORDAN, DORCAS, of Cople, 25 Oct. 1708; 24 Nov. 1708.
Grandson Patrick son of Alex. Spence, gent. decd.; to Jordan Weedon and his sister Mary Weedon now wife to the son of Bunch Roe; to Dorcas Sanford dau. of my eldest dau. Elizabeth Sturman; dau. Jane Spence; dau. Ellenor Munroe; friends John Sturman, John Higgins and Law. Pope exors.; to Wm. Moxle Snr.; to Samuel Gray, clerk; to Jemima Pope, Anna Sturman Snr.; Anna Sturman Jrn.; son in law John Sturman.

PRICE, MERIDAY, 14 April 1708; 24 Nov. 1708.
Son Thomas; son in law John Butler; dau. Mary Cole; dau. Grace; sons Meriday and John; dau. Katherine.
Inv. of William Ruch, 23 Feb. 1708.

BOOTH, ELIZABETH, 27 Oct. 1708; 26 Jan. 1708.
Dau. Ann Grimstead her husband Thomas, and their sons William and Thomas Grimestead; to Joan Stephens; son in law Edward Mazengo; grandchildren Sarah and John Mazengo; son in law Thomas Grimstead exor.

COCHREN, CHRISTIAN, 26 Oct. 1708; 23 Feb. 1708.
Dau. Elizabeth Cochren all estate.

BUTLER, CALEB, 16 Feb. 1708-9; 25 May 1709.
Wife Mary; dau. Jane; son in law Robert Vaulx and his decd. uncle John Foxhall; Sarah Elliott dau. of Sarah Elliott and her decd. uncle John Foxhall; son in law James Vaulx; my sister Anne wife of John Bayley; to Thomas Robins; to Mary Butler dau. of John Butler decd.; to Thomas Clayton, Snr.; to Thomas Boyleston; sister Sarah Elliott widow; to Jenny wife of Thomas Shaw; to Elizabeth wife of Capt. Richard Craddock; friend James Taylor.
Inv. of Manuel Ham, 21 March 1708.

WILLIAM HARPER, 14 July 1709; 28 Sept. 1709.
To Colonel Allerton; to cousins William and Thomas Harper all estate.

BOOK V.

GERRARD, JOHN, ———; 25 Apl. 1711.
My brother in law William Newton and his wife Barbara; my brother in law William Davis and Elizabeth his wife; my wife Jane; my mother Elizabeth Johnson; my brother James Johnson; my sisters Frances and Anne Johnson.
Inv. of Mr. John Higgins by Augt. Higgins—1712.

HORE, JOHN, Wash. Par. 16 Feb. 1711; 26 March 1712.
Son Elias land in Stafford; son John plant, where I now live; son James land on so. side of Mattox creek which I bought of John Beard and Mary his wife; until my children come of age; exors. sons John and Elias.
Inv. of William Rush, by Elizabeth Rush, 6 Apl. 1712.
Inv. of James Vaulx 23, Feb. 1711.
Inv of John Cole 8 July 1712.
Inv. of Charles Dunkan by Frances Dunkan, 8 July 1712.

EDWARDS, MERIDA, 17 June 1712; 27 Aug. 1712.
Son John exor.; my wife Ann; son William; son Thomas; my granddaughter: godson John Maders; daughter Ellenor.
Inv. of William Offile 23 Aug. 1712.

ARRINGTON, JOHN, 20 April 1712; 24 Sept. 1712.
Wife Susanna; dau. Mildred Arrington; brother Thos. and my wife exors.
Inv. of Benjamin Weedon by Susanna Weedon 7 Oct. 1712.
Inv. of John Brown by Mary Brown 26 Nov. 1712.

LANCELOTT, JOHN, 21 Aug. 1706; 28 Jan. 1712.
To coz. John Lancelott my two plantations one formerly my brother William's and the other that which Gilbert Atwood now lives on but his mother Jane Lancelott to live on it during her life; in case John Lancelott dies then to his sister my coz. Jane Simmons failing which to my coz. William Butler and——; to my wife Mary remainder of estate; brother William's children.

BUTLER, JOHN, ———; 28 Jan. 1712.
To George Purvis; to Wm. Cutler; Richard Coggin; wife Kath. and my children; wife and bro. Wm. Butler exors.; eldest son Thomas; sons John and James; my brother James Butler.

NEWTON, ROSE, 1 Dec. 1712; 4 Feb. 1712.
To son Thomas land in Va. and Md.; my late husband Thomas Gerrard.

BLANCHFLOWER, TEMPERANCE, 12 Dec. 1711; 4 Feb. 1712.
To Ann Davis when 17; son Osman Crabb; my grandchildren the children of my two sons Gerard Hutt and Osman Crabb, the two latter to be exors.
Inv. of Robert Hore by Sarah Hore, 28 Jan. 1712.
Inv. of George Hardwick, 25 March 1713.
A/c of estate of Capt. Law. Washington 1698; Rec. 3 April 1713.

GARNER, JOHN, 3 Feb. 1712; 4 April 1713.
Land in Northumberland to son William; sons Abraham, John, Joseph and Jeremiah; dau. Jane Joyce; dau. Susannah Garner; son William 500 acres in Stafford; my loving wife.

COX, VINCENT, 3 Feb. 1712; 1 April 1713.
Dau. Winifred Cox under 21 and to her a diamond ring that was her mother's, she to be under the care of my wife Jane and latter extx. daughter Ann.
Inv. of James Moore by Ann Moore, 5 June 1713.

JONES, JOHN, 10 Jan. 1707; 5 June 1713.
Son Nathaniel; dau. Elizabeth Jones; dau. Sarah Jones; son Charles to John son of William Overall; to Mary Overall; dau. Anne Jones; my wife; Wm. Overall exor.

HINDMER, JOHN, 2 Dec. 1712; 5 Jan. 1713.
Grandson Hindmer Shephard when 10 years; his mother my dau. Ann Shephard to be extx.

MOORE, THOMAS, 5 Feb. 1709; 5 Jan. 1713.
Sons William and Thomas; to Margaret Moore when 18; wife Margt. extx.
Inv. of Mr. Thomas Marson, 5 June 1713.
Inv. of Robert Fletcher by Ellenor Jennings, 5 June 1713.
Inv. of Capt. Richard Cradock, 6 June 1713.
Inv. of William Garland by George Garland, 6 June 1713.

MARKHAM, LEWIS, 15 March 1712-3; 13 June 1713.
To Joseph Bayley and his wife Ann; my children; wife Elizabeth and Joseph Bayley exors.

ATWELL, JOHN, 6 April 1713; 30 June 1713.
Sons Thomas, Youell and Samuel, sons are under 21; my three daus. Hannah, Lydia and Frances Atwell; wife Elizabeth extx.

CLEMENS, DAVID, 10 Dec. 1711; 30 June 1713.
Wife Isabella; dau. Sarah Beard; dau. Grace Downton; dau. Susanna Arrington.
Inv. of John Jones sworn before Capt. Benj. Berryman, 24 June 1713.
Inv. of Edward Wood, 3 July 1713.
Inv. of Thomas Charles sworn before Major Henry Ashton, 24 June 1713.
Inv. of William Watts, 3 July 1713.
Inv. of John Henmons, 7 Aug. 1713.
Inv. of James Haselrigg by Richd. Haselrigg, 7 Aug. 1713.
Inv. of Major Francis Wright, gent., by Martha Wright, 7 Aug. 1713.

BAGGE, MARY, wife of John Bagge, clerk, 2 Feb. 1712; 5 Sept. 1713.
Mentions marriage articles between her and her husband of date 19 Dec. 1711; my dau. Jane Butler and my late husband Caleb Butler; son Robert Vaulx and his dau. Mary; son John Duddlestone; dau. Elizabeth Porten; Mr. Daniel Porten; husband John Bagge; to James son of Elizabeth and John Jarvis; to Wm. Moxley, Snr.
Inv. of John Atwell by Eliz. Atwell, 5 Sept. 1713.
Inv. of Mr. John Washington, gent., by Nathl. Washington, 5 Sept. 1713.

HARRISON, GEORGE, 2 Oct. 1713; 10 Dec. 1713.
Sons Thomas, George, John, William, James, Peter and Willoughby Harrison.

MORRIS, JOHN, Nuncp. will, 13 Nov. 1713; 24 Feb. 1713.
To William son of John Collin; to Vincent son of William Wyatt; wife Elizabeth extx.

HEADLEY, ANN, 22 July 1713; 25 Nov. 1713.
Sons Robert, William, Henry; daughters Barbary Webb, Eliz. Headley and Ann Headley; son John.

NEALE, DANIEL, gent., 19 Dec. 1713; 2 March 1713.
Dau. Hannah Neale; son Presley, Daniel, Christopher and Rodham; wife Ursual extx; dau. Frances Neale.

WILSON, HENRY, 10 Feb. 1713-4; 2 March 1713.
Dau. Ann Wilson; exor Rich'd. Vanlendgen.
Inv. of John Curtis, 3 March 1713.

SMITH, JAMES, 9 Dec. 1713; 9 April 1714.
Son James when 20; wife Ann; my three daus. Jane, Ann and Eliz. Smith.
Inv. of Alex. Cahoe, 31 March 1714.
Inv. of George Wattey, 31 March 1714.
Inv. of William Williams, 31 March 1714.
Inv. of John Tancell, 31 March 1714.
Inv. of William Willis, 31 March 1714.
Inv. of Thomas Powell, 31 March 1714.
Inv. of William Brown by Hester Brown, 26 May 1714.

MUNROE, ANDREW, gent., 30 Dec. 1713; 9 June 1714.
Son Spence; brother William Munroe; son Andrew; dau. Susannah Munroe; to Andrew son of my brother William; dau. Elizabeth Arrington and her son John; my wife Sarah; son in law William Elliott; dau. in law Elizabeth Elliott; to Thomas Mustin; friends Charles Tyler and Richard Watts and brother William Munroe, exors.

SMITH, CHARLES, Par. of Sittenburn; 16 Feb. 1709; 9 June 1714.
Son William and dau. Mary Smith; son Francis; wife Ann; Nathl. Pope, Snr., and Mr. Joseph Bayley trustees.

WRIGHT, JOHN, Cople, Par. 21 Jan. 1713; 9 June 1714.
Grandson Thomas son of my dau. Hester; granddau. Mary dau. of my dau. Susanna; my son John and the child my wife goes with land in Richmond county; to Anna dau. of Thomas and Elizabeth Sorrell; son Thomas Blundell and my brother Thomas Walker, trustees.
Inv. of John Gray, 28 July 1714.
Inv. of Daniel Carroll by Mary Carroll, 28 July 1714.

BUTLER, THOMAS, 2 May 1714; 2 Sept. 1714.
Sons William and James; dau. Elizabeth Baker; grandson Thomas son of John Butler near where Kath. Butler lives; to John and James sons of James Butler; to Ann Baker dau. of Elizabeth Baker; to dau. Elizabeth all her mother's clothes; exors. sons James and John.
Inv. of James Butler, 29 Sept. 1714.
Inv. of John Butler, 28 Nov. 1714.
Inv. of Thomas Butler by James Butler and John Baker, 29 Sept. 1714.

PRATT, JOHN, 20 Sept. 1714; 30 Nov. 1714.
Granddau. Margarte Pratt; grandson John Lovell; dau. in law Mrs. Mary Pease; son John Pratt.

ALDERSON, GEORGE, 10 Nov. 1714; 3 Dec. 1714.
Daughters Jane, Mary and Margaret Alderson; my mother Mary Baxter; daus. under 16 years of age; mother and dau. Jane exors.
Inv. of Nicholas Luke, 26 Jan. 1714.
Inv. of Pierce Gower, 26 Jan. 1714.
Inv. of Bryant Murphy, 27 Apl. 1715.
Inv. of Caleb Butler, 27 Apl. 1715.
Inv. of Gilbert Atwood, 27 Apl. 1715.
Inv. of Benjamin Eattle, 27 Apl. 1715.
Inv. of Katherine Bonam, 25 May 1715.

LEE, RICHARD, Cople Par., 3 Mch. 1714; 27 Apl. 1715.
To eldest son Richard the land granted to my father in the year 1650; to son Henry; to son Philip land in Maryland; son Francis; son Thomas land in Northumberland; dau. Ann Fitzhugh land in Stafford; exors. Richard, Thomas and Henry Lee.

JOHNSON, JAMES, 9 Feb. 1714; 10 Jan. 1715.

To my mother during her life the land left to me by my brother John Gerrard and after her death to my godson Gerrard Davies; sister Ann Johnson; godson John Newton; coz. Eliza. Wigginton; coz. William son of William Davies; friend John Footman; to John Hines; to John Hardy; extx. mother Elizabeth Johnson.

MARREAN, DANIEL, 7 Aug. 1712; 10 Jan. 1715.

Sons John and William; dau. Hester; wife Elizabeth extx.

ARRINGTON, THOMAS, 16 Oct. 1715; 8 Dec. 1715.

Wife Elizabeth; son John; brother Wansford Arrington; daus. Dorcas and Jane; son Thomas.

THOMPSON, THOMAS, gent., 17 Jan. 1715; 28 Mch. 1716.

My two daus. Alice and Anna Thompson at 20 years; friends Thomas Lee and William Pierce; friend Edward Ransdell; son in law Patrick Spence; son in law Thomas Spence; to Elizabeth Colson; dau. Anna to live with Mrs. Sibella wife of Wm. Pierce.

FENN, THOMAS, 30 Jan. 1715; 28 Mch. 1716.

Friend Morris Hurley when she comes to 16 years; dau. Elizabeth at 16; to Mary Couch; to Daniel Conniers; to Thos. Lankford; Terrence Conniers exor.

CARDWELL, RICHARD, 4 Dec. 1715; 30 May 1716.

Wife Mary; son Richard at 21; daus. Margaret and Winifred.

WALKER, THOMAS, 6 Jan. 1715; 30 May 1716.

Sons Thomas, George, Edmund and Samuel; wife Mary; daus. Margery and Ann; to John and Thomas Wright; daus. Mary and Rachel; son Benjamin.

WESTCOMB, JAMES, gent., 27 June 1714; 30 May 1716.

To servant Judith Laycock; friend Mary Collins alias Collier, extx.

ERWIN, JOHN, 10 April 1716; 30 May 1716.

My godchildren John son of George and Anne South; Frances dau. of John Sorrell and Anne his late wife; Jemimah dau. of John and Hannah Awbrey; John son of John and Frances Awbrey; John son of Charles and Temperance Lucas and Elizabeth dau. of Thomas and Elizabeth Sorrell, all to have 2 years' schooling each; to William Clark my overseer; friends John Awbrey and Thomas Sorrell exors.

SMITH, ANNE, 16 Jan. 1715; 30 May 1716.

To Alice Beckwith; dau. in law Mary Smith extx. Probated by Mary Gerrard the extx.

Inv. of John Howard at house of Susanna Howard, 30 May 1716.

Inv. of Susanna Garner by son Benj. Garner, 30 May 1716.

Inv. of John Hobson of Cople, 30 May 1716.

Inv. of Charles Walker at house of Elizabeth Walker, 30 May 1716.

REDMAN, FRANCIS, 16 Apl. 1716; 25 July 1716.

To Mary Lambert; to James son of Robert Lovell; to Israel Chapman; exor. kinsman Robert Lovell.

BEARD, THOMAS, ———; 25 July 1716.
    All estate to cousin Lovell Massey and Mary Lovell.

CROUTCHMAN, JOHN, ———; 25 July 1716.
    To wife Sarah all estate.
Inv. of John Waters, 25 July 1716.
Inv. of Sutton Roe, 25 July 1716.
Inv. of Anne Smith at house of William Gerard, signed by Mary Gerrard, 25 July 1716.

WHEELER, THOMAS, planter, 30 Dec. 1715; 29 Aug. 1716.
    To sisters Mary Thornbury and Elizabeth Hicking; to Samuel son of William Wheeler; to Anne Gough and her husband Robert; my two brothers William Wheeler and Samuel Thornbury; exor. Joseph Bayley.

BOOK VI.

BAXTER, Mary, widow; 5 Oct. 1716; 31 Oct. 1716.
    The estate that is in my hands that belongs to the orphans of George Alderson; son Thomas; dau. Anne; granddau. Jane Alderson; dau. Mary; granddau. Ann; sons Abraham, Thomas and William.

WORDEN, JOHN, physician, 17 Jan. 1714; 31 Oct. 1716.
    Godson Worden Pope; friend Nathaniel Pope; Joseph Weeks; Jane wife of Nathl. Pope.

SPEED, RALPH, planter, 13 Sept. 1716; 31 Oct. 1716.
    All estate to friend Abraham Griffen.

WATTS, RICHARD, 23 Apl. 1715; 31 Oct. 1716.
    Sons Richard and John plantation where my mother does live; my five children; wife Mary extx.

BLAGG, ABRAHAM, 6 Oct. 1716; 28 Nov. 1716.
    Mother Margaret Blagg extx.; son Abraham; my brother Richard Watt's children; personal estate to son and my wife.

MANLEY, WILLIAM, 30 May 1716; 28 Nov. 1716.
    Wife Penelope; daus. Penelope and Jemima; son John.

SHEADRICK, THOMAS, 29 Apl. 1716; 28 Nov. 1716.
    My three children to be of age at 16; eldest son John; son Thomas; wife and my brother Abraham Ethell exors.

PORTEN, DANIEL, 31 Oct. 1714; 19 Nov. 1716.
    To Mary Furlong dau. of my sister Anne Furlong; son Cradock Porten; father in law Major Samuel Boush exor.; wife Elizabeth.

RAWLINGS, ANTHONY, 21 Apl. 1713; 28 Nov. 1716.
    Wife Martha; two sons Richard and Samuel.
Inv. of William Graham, 28 Nov. 1716.

DOWNING, RALPH, 10 Aug. 1716; 30 Jan. 1716.
    Friend Mr. John Chilton; brother in law Samuel Houell; sister Ruth Houell extx.

WEEKES, JOSEPH, 4 Jan. 1716; 30 Jan. 1716.
Wife Mary; dau. Sarah; my two eldest children Sarah and William.

WELCH, GARRATT, 9 Sept. 1709; 30 Jan. 1716.
Friend John Pratt, Jr., exor.

OCCANY, DANIEL, planter, 27 Feb. 1715; 30 Jan. 1716.
Grandson Daniel Crabb; to John Crabb; to grandson John Crabb and my son
in law Thomas Sorrell; friend Willoughby Allerton and Henry Lee exors.

HAVEN, STEPHEN, 13 Jan. 1716; 30 Jan. 1716.
Son Arthur all my estate in Ireland and Gt. Britain; dau. Elizabeth Haven;
extx. Margaret Herra and friend Geo. Eskridge to assist her.
Inv. of Brookes Abbington, 6 Feb. 1716.

BRYANT, WILLIAM, 23 Jan. 1716; 27 Feb. 1716.
Dau. Sarah; son William; my daughters; exors. Richard Walls and his wife
Mary.

BATEMAN, WILLIAM, 18 Feb. 1716; 27 Feb. 1716.
Eldest dau. Mary; 2nd dau. Elizabeth; 3rd dau. Sarah; son John; wife Elizabeth extx.

ROBERTSON, PRISCILLA, 8 Jan. 1716; 27 Mch. 1717.
Dau. Mary Robertson; exor. William Humphreys.

SELF, ROBERT, 18 June 1716; 27 Mch. 1717.
Son John; wife Jane extx.

HEADLEY, JOHN, 15 Dec. 1716; 26 June 1717.
Wife Frances all my estate.

SHAW, THOMAS, 5 Mch. 1716; 26 June 1717.
Son Thomas; wife Jane; bro. in law John Elliott.

MOON, JOHN, 10 June 1717; 26 June 1717.
Son John; to Eliz. Hawley my wife's granddaughter; wife Elizabeth.
Inv. of Charles Chilton, 26 June 1717.
Inv. of Mr. Henry Netherton, 26 June 1717.
Inv. of William Robottom, 25 July 1717.

SUMMERVILLE, JOHN, 9 June 1717; 28 Aug. 1717.
Wife Mary land in Stafford; son in law William Thompson; dau. in law
Susanna Thompsan; son in law John Watts; to William Sturman.

PARSONS, DOROTHY, 16 Feb. 1716; 28 Aug. 1717.
Dau. Mary Finch; son in law John Finch and his son John; granddau. Ann;
grandson Lawrence Abbington; son James Abbington; son John Parsons;
son Joseph Parsons; dau. Mary Nicholls.
Inv. of Robert Jones, 12 Sept. 1717.
Inv. of Susanna Howard, 13 Sept. 1717.
Inv. of John Jenkins, 13 Sept. 1717.
Inv. of Richard Watts, 13 Sept. 1717.
Inv. of Thomas Shaw by Jane Shaw, 15 Oct. 1717.

NEWGENT, ELIAS, 14 Oct. 1717; 27 Nov. 1717.
All estate to Robert Vaulx.

PRICE, THOMAS, 3 Sept. 1717; 27 Nov. 1717.
Wife Margaret; eldest son William; son Thomas; son Merida; son John; dau. Susanna Price; son William; brother Merida Price.

WATERS, DOROTHY, 6 Nov. 1717; 27 Nov. 1717.
Dau. Sarah Williams; dau. Sarah Owen; dau. Ann Dunkan; son Blanchflower Dunkan; to Henry and Jarrett sons of John Medford; son William Macclanacon exor.

QUISENBERRY, JOHN, 23 Nov. 1714; 27 Nov. 1717.
Son William; son Humphrey; wife Ann Extx. Witnessed by Francis Quisenberry.

GILBERT, MICHAEL, 2 Oct. 1717; 27 Nov. 1717.
Sons William, John and Michael; grandson William Shortridge; wife Jane and son William exors.

BAYLEY, JOSEPH, 5 Dec. 1717; 29 Jan. 1717.
My brother Michael and his son Thomas Bayley; goddaughter Mary Butler; wife Anne extx.

BONAM, THOMAS, gent., 18 Nov. 1717; 29 Jan. 1717.
To Sarah Baker dau. of John Baker; my decd. wife; to brother Capt. George Eskridge; to friend Thomas Sorrell; nephew Samuel Bonam; nephews Daniel Bonam and Phillip Bonam.
Inv. of Robert Sparrow, 17 Feb. 1717.

RUST, SAMUEL, 16 Aug. 1717; 26 Mch. 1718.
To Mr. Patrick Spence and his father in law Capt. George Eskridge; sons Peter, John and Mathew Rust; sons George, William and Benj. Rust; dau. Ann Harrison; dau. Hannah Rust; wife Martha and son Jeremiah Rust exors.

ROLLINS, WILLIAM, 4 Dec. 1717; 26 Mch. 1718.
To Sarah Sebastin; my three children Philip, Mary and Thomas Rollins; eldest son is 12 next Nov.; dau. 9 Jan. ensuing, youngest son 7 in March ensuing.

GARNER, BENJAMIN, 31 Mch. 1718; 28 May 1718.
Brother Parish Garner; coz. Henry Garner; coz. Thomas son of Henry Garner; coz. Joseph son of John Garner; godson Benj. Walker; coz. Vincent Lewis son of William Lewis; brother Thomas Garner; sister Mary Price; sister Martha; coz. James son of James Garner; coz. John Garner; brother James Garner exor.

STONE, THOMAS, 31 Mch. 1718; 28 May 1718.
Friend Robert Barnard exor.
Inv. of John Marloe, 28 May 1718.
Inv. of Arthur King, 28 May 1718.

BENNETT, COSSOM, 25 June 1718; 18 July 1718.
Wife Katherine; daus. Lucy and Susan; sons William and Cossom; Mr. Dade Massey, trustee.

ALLWORTHY, ROBERT (nuncp.), 25 June 1718; 10 July 1718.
Estate to wife Ruth.

SMITH, JOSEPH, 13 May 1718; 25 June 1718.
Son Nathaniel; son Joseph; daus. Mary and Joyce Smith.

PALMER, SARAH, 2 Mch. 1717; 25 June 1718.
Dau. Sarah wife of Edward Turner; granddaus. Sarah and Jane Turner.

HEMMINGS, JOSEPH (Nuncp.), 25 June 1718; 10 July 1718.
To godson John Jones; wife Elizabeth.

WIGGINTON, ROGER, 3 Mch. 1717; 14 Aug. 1718.
Sons William and Roger; daus. Elizabeth and Ann Wigginton; son Henry;
brother William Wigginton and Willoughby Allerton exors.

THOMAS, HUGH, 6 Nov. 1717; 14 Aug. 1718.
Two sons Daniel and Hugh; brother John Thomas; wife Ann extx.

MUCKLEROY, ELIZABETH, 12 Feb. 1717; 14 Aug. 1718.
Granddau. Elizabeth Pope dau. of John and Elizabeth Pope; Jemima dau.
of my son Lawrence Pope and his wife Jemima; grandson Thomas Youel son
of Harman and Dinah Youell; granddau. Elizabeth dau. of the same; dau.
Dinah Youell and husband Harman exors.

ALLEN, WILLIAM, 31 Mch. 1718; 30 July 1718.
Son William who was born 21 Oct. 1704; exor. James Courtwell.
Inv. of Brooks Mottershead, 15 Aug. 1718.
Inv. of Thomas Spellman, 15 Aug. 1718.

CLAYTOR, THOMAS, 23 July 1718; 18 Oct. 1718.
Grandson Thomas son of William Claytor; son Thomas and my wife Katherine exors.

HIGDON, JOHN, 7 Sept. 1718; 21 Oct. 1718.
Sons Daniel and John.

POTTER, WILLIAM, ———; 4 Nov. 1718.
Wife Frances; sons John and James; dau. Frances.

WARD, JOHN, 30 Aug. 1718; 4 Nov. 1718.
Son Henry; son in law James Brisco; dau. Jane Ward extx.
Inv. of Edmund Owen, 23 Aug. 1718.

McBOYD, PATRICK, 13 May 1718; 29 Dec. 1718.
Son Thomas; wife Mary; David Conner and coz. Carran Branham exors.

HARDWICK, WILLIAM, 31 Oct. 1718; 10 Mch. 1718.
Wife Eliza; son James; dau. Frances; son George; dau. Dorcas.

VEEL, JOHN, 20 Nov. ———; 10 Mch. 1718.
Land in Stafford to sons John and Morris; dau. Susan; wife Deliverance
extx.; brother Humphrey Pope and Caudry Vaughan trustees.
Inv. of Peter Eaton, 7 Mch. 1719.

KENNER, RICHARD, 17 Nov. 1718; 10 Jan. 1719.
To son Winder Kenner land where Mr. Wm. Chandler now lives; son Richard; brother John Kenner; son Rodham; wife Elizabeth; mother in law Elizabeth Winder; daus. Elizabeth and Frances Kenner; exors. Major Henry Ashton and John Awbury.

WILLSON, JOHN, 22 July 1718; 10 June 1719.
Wife Mary; children Allen, John, William, Sarah and the child my wife goes with.

BATCHELLOR, THOMAS, planter, 15 Apl. 1719; 3 Aug. 1719.
Grandson John Morton; dau. Anne Morton; wife Mary extx.
Inv. of Abraham Anderson, 3 Aug. 1719.
Inv. of James Lane, 3 Aug. 1719.
Inv. of Solomon Redman, 4 Aug. 1719.

MASON, WILLIAM, 23 Sept. 1719; 16 Dec. 1719.
Estate to William Jennings.
Inv. of William Lewis 30 Sept. 1719.
Inv. of Ann Thomas, 16 Dec. 1719.
Inv. of Dorcas Carter, 8 Mch. 1719.

CRABB, OSMAN, 25 Jan. 1719; ——— Mch. 1719.
Sons Osman, Gerrard, Daniel and John; dau. Lettice; wife Sarah extx. and bro. in law Thomas Sorrell trustee.
Inv. of Thomas Woodier, 9 Mch. 1719.
Inv. of Nathl. Pope, gent., 9 Mch. 1719.

BUSHROD, JOHN, 26 Jan. 1719; 30 Mch. 1720.
Daughters Apphia Fauntleroy and Eliz. Meriwether; dau. Hannah Bushrod when 17; dau. Sarah when 17; son Richard; son John when 19; son Thomas; wife Hannah extx.

GIBSON, BEHETHLAND, 20 Aug. 1716; 30 Mch. 1720.
Grandsons Dade Massey and William Storke.

KELLEY, WILLIAM, 17 Nov. 1719; 12 April 1720.
The child my wife Ann now goes with; dau. Dorothy Anderson; exors. Lawrence Butler and Jarrat Ford.

BOOK VII.

DRISKALL, DARBY, 11 May 1720; 8 July 1720.
To Mrs. Kath. McCarty and to Capt. Daniel McCarty; to Robert Bayley; to John Gore; to David Williamson; to Edward Clark.

FIELD, DANIEL, 17 Apl. 1720; ——— July 1720.
Dau. Joyce Hudson; to Emma Price; sons Abraham and Henry exors.; son John Wheeler and Evan Price.

POWER, ROBERT, 26 Mch. 1720; ——— July 1720.
Dau. in law Ursual Whiting at 16 years; to Lovell Massie; goddau. Philander Davis; wife Hannah; son in law William Whiting; exors. wife and Robert Lovell.

28

MARTIN, JOHN, ———; 29 June 1720.
Brother William Martin and his son John; sister Eliz. Smith; to Eliz. Collins; friend William Wyatt; to Vincent and Mathew Wyatt; to John Morris son of James Dunn; to Jane Dunn; exor. brother William.

HIGDON, JOHN, 28 Apl. 1720; 29 June 1720.
Son John; brother Daniel Higdon; wife Magdalene extx.
Inv. of Augustine Higgins, gent., 9 July 1721.

SPENCER, FRANCIS, of Cople, gent., 3 Dec. 1715; ——— July 1720.
To my brother John's dau. Frances Spencer; to Rev. James Breechin; friend Daniel McCarty exor; to George Eskridge, Jr.

ROBINSON, THOMAS, 22 Apl. 1717; 4 Aug. 1720.
Daughters Mary, Elizabeth and Susanna; son Thomas and his children.

SOUTH, GEORGE, 29 Feb. 1719; 13 Sept. 1720.
Son George begot by me on the body of Ann my wife late wife of Isaac Shepherd; son John begot on same; dau. Hannah; my son's godfather Thomas Lambert; exors. John and James Awbury.

SUTHERLAND, JOHN, 1 Apl. 1720; 13 Sept. 1720.
Wife's oldest and youngest son; wife Katherine; dau. Catherine.

CLAYTER, KATHERINE, 22 June 1720; 6 Oct. 1720.
Son Thomas, dau. Jane Carter; dau. Ann Goff and grandson Thomas Clayter exors.

BYARD, JAMES, 6 Sept. 1720; tailor; 6 Oct. 1720.
Son John exor.; dau. Sarah Byard; wife Mary.
Inv. of James Butler, 7 Oct. 1720.
Inv. of Jonas Handley, 8 Dec. 1720.
Inv. of John Longworth, 8 Sept. 1722.

TUCKER, ELIZABETH, 3 May 1722; ——— Oct. 1722.
Dau. Mary Woodward; dau. Sarah Minor; dau. Rebecca Tucker; sons Benj.; Joseph, John and Henry.
Inv. of Joseph Taylor, 24 Aug. 1722.

SPILLER, DOROTHY, 20 Apl. 1722; ——— Nov. 1722.
To William son of Benj. Berryman; granddaughters Verlinda and Jane and grandson John; exor. Benj. Berryman.

Inv. of John Gammon, 9 Nov. 1722.
Inv. of John Pope, 9 Feb. 1722.
Inv. of Richard Bell, 5 Mch. 1722.

SANDERS, PHILLIP, 9 Dec. 1722; 6 Apl. 1723.
Son William; dau. Urslee Taylor; grandson John son of William Sander grandson Phillip; granddau. Mary Sanders; wife Elizabeth.
Inv. of John Muse, 6 Apl. 1723.

POPE, LAWRENCE, 23 Mch. 1723; 10 May 1723.
Sons Humphrey, Thomas and John; dau. Elizabeth; dau. Ann; dau. Mary; dau. Penelope; dau. Catherine; to James son of Benj. Waddey; godson John son of Nicholas Minor; wife Jemima; brother Humphrey Pope and brother Nicholas Minor; wife and son Humphrey exors.

COLEMAN, JAMES, 22 Mch. 1722; 10 May 1723.
Wife Jane; two elder sons James and John; son Richard; son James Lewis; after decease of my sons mother in law; son in law Joseph Carr; to Martha Sparrow; to Elizabeth Carr.
Inv. of William Kitching at house of Eliz. Kitching, 5 May 1723.

VAULX, JAMES, 16 Oct. 1710; 6 Sept. 1711.
To James son of Elizabeth Field; my brother and sister Richard and Elizabeth Cradock; to Capt. Richard Cradock; to sister Jane Butler the silver hilted sword of my father Butler; to Mary Baxter; to Joseph Merker; exor. brother Robert Vaulx.

ROWLAND, DAVID, 28 June 1711, 6 Sept. 1711.
To Bryant Brannen; to Edward Hoburd; to Rebecca Dab.
Inv. of the estate of Susanna Gerrard, 29 Aug. 1711.
Inv. of estate of Mr. John Gerrard at the house of Mrs. Jane Gerrard, 7 Sept. 1711.
(Editor's note. The above four entries are not recorded in the book for year 1711.)

VAULX, (Capt.) ROBERT, 30 Nov. 1721; 5 Dec. 1721.
Sons Robert and James; my wife and my three children (third child is not named); wife Elizabeth, Augustine Washington and Richard Kenner exors.

RAMERY, JACOB, Snr., 17 July 1702; 5 Dec. 1721.
Wife Mary; youngest son Jacob; eldest son William.
Inv. of William Brown, Jr., 11 July 1723.

DAMAVORELL, SAMUEL, 12 April 1723; 8 Aug. 1723.
Son Samuel; dau. Magdalene Rust; dau. Elizabeth Harrison; wife Hannah.

JENKINS, THOMAS, 9 Dec. 1722; 8 Aug. 1723.
Son Jeremiah at 19, he to stay with his mother in law until then; wife Elizabeth extx.

LUTTRELL, SIMON, 1 Aug. 1723; 8 Oct. 1723.
Sons Simon and John; dau. Margaret Luttrell; wife Elizabeth extx.

MUSE, JOHN, 5 Apl. 1723; 8 Oct. 1723.
To son Thomas one shilling; dau. Jane Pritchett one shilling; dau. Ann Willson one shilling; dau. Mary Quisenberry one shilling; rest of estate to dau. in law Ann Muse.
Inv. of John Allerton Eales, 6 July 1721.
Inv. of Elizabeth Murphy, 6 July 1721.

FROUD, JOHN, 4 Mch. 1717; 1 Aug. 1721.
Dau. Jane Lamkin; granddaughter Winifred Lamkin at 18; wife Winifred.
Inv. of Thomas Watson, 1 Aug. 1721.

BAKER, SUSANNAH, 23 July 1721; 6 Sept. 1721.
To John Steel; to John Keesee 50 acres which I had by my husband John Baker; to John Gannack.
Inv. of Hanlett Golding, 30 Aug. 1721.

BREECHIN, JAMES, 19 Oct. 1721; 6 Apl. 1722.
My late wife Ann; sons William and James; to Mr. John Rele; to Dennis Lynsey; to Thomas Poindexter; daus. Anna and Jane; to James and Anna Sorrell; wife Sarah; kinsman Thomas Sorrell; wife and Capt. George Turberville exors.

WIGGINGTON, WILLIAM, 7 Nov. 1721; ——— Mch. 1721.
Son James Johnson Wiggington; dau. Elizabeth Wiggington; wife Frances. Mentions brother Henry Wigginton if he should come to Virginia.

ONEAL, GARRETT, 3 Apl. 1722; 7 May 1722.
Daughter in law Elizabeth Butler; sons Garrett and John; dau. Ellenor Oneal; my four daughters when 18; exor. friend Henry Washington.

DUDLEY, MARY, 20 Apl. 1722; 7 May 1722.
Son John Collins; granddaughter Mary Collins.

NEWTON, WILLIAM, 1 Mch. 1721; 4 Jan. 1722.
Son John land in Westmoreland and in King George also land in Gt. Britain; son Benjamin; wife Elizabeth; daughters Frances, Sarah and Elizabeth Newton.

BOOK VIII.

STURMAN, JOHN, aged 73 years, ———; 27 Nov. 1723.
Wife Anna; son John and godson Dick; son Thomas; daughter Neale; dau. Dorcas Sanford; son William; dau. Jemimah Stone.

BALL, ROBERT, 29 May 1723; 9 Dec. 1723.
Sons Robert, George, Emanuel and Gerrard Ball; dau. Sarah Ball, my wife and children Daniel and Benoni; to Ralph Elston; brother Gerrard Ball of Maryland exor.

REED, JOHN, 3 Jan. 1723; 10 Mch. 1723.
My four sons John, William, Clayter and Thomas; dau. Mary Reed; wife Jane and Giles Carter exors.

BAKER, THOMAS, 31 Jan. 1723; 10 Mch. 1723.
Estate to John Jewell, Snr.

DAVIS, ELIZABETH, widow, relict of William Davis, 6 Feb. 1723; 10 Mch. 1723.
Son William; dau. Elizabeth Davis; my four other daughters Frances, Sarah, Barbara and Ann; son Gerrard Davis; son William exor.

ALLERTON, WILLOUGHBY, gent., 17 Jan. 1723; 8 Apl. 1724.
Wife Hannah, to my wife's daughters Hannah and Sarah Bushrod; son Isaac; dau. Elizabeth Allerton; son exor.

McCARTY, DANIEL, 29 Mch. 1724; 9 June 1724.

Son Dennis all land in Stafford; son Billington; son Thaddeus; son Daniel lands in Westmoreland; to son Billington lands in Farnham, Richmond co., that was my grandfather Billington's land; son Thaddeus land in Richmond that was Capt. John Rice's land; land in Northumberland to Billington; daughters Winifred and Sarah; dau. Mrs. Anna Barbara Fitzhugh; to each of my grandchildren; to son Mr. Henry Fitzhugh; my son Daniel under care of Mr. John Gilpin of Whitehaven to be continued until his education comes to one hundred pounds to be paid on his arrival in Virginia; son in law William Payne; pictures of son and dau. Fitzhugh to their son when 7 years old, but the pictures of myself and first wife to remain in my dwelling house; exors. in trust Col. John Tayloe, Humphrey Pope, Nicholas Minor, John Fitzhugh and Samuel Peachey, gents., until son Thaddeus be 17; my first wife's daughters Elizabeth Sherman and Mary Burns; my uncle Mr. Joseph Taylor late clerk of Lancaster; to my aunt Mrs. Barbara Tayloe during her life; my brothers Philip, Francis, Thomas and Henry Lee; friend Capt. Eskridge; my wife Anna and her brothers Col. and Capt. Lee.

RANSDELL, EDWARD, 1 May 1724; 24 June 1724.

Eldest son Wharton; sons John and Edward; my wife's plantation in Rappahannock; wife Amy the estate which formerly did belong to her first husband Capt. John Kelley; the orphan of Capt. John Kelley; to Elizabeth Jeffreys; dau. in law Mary Kelley; to Nicholas Stephens; daughters Elizabeth Talbott and Milicent Longworth; to William Longworth; son Wharton exor.

ASHTON, CHARLES, 9 Sept. 1724; 30 Sept. 1724.

Eldest son John; youngest sons Charles and Burdett; dau. Jane to be educated by her aunt Storke; brother Burdett Ashton exor.

BROWN, GEORGE, 18 May 1724; 20 July 1724.

Nephew John son of brother William Brown, decd.; to Thomas son of my brother Thomas Brown; to George son of George During; to John Fryer; to George son of William and Elizabeth Hardage, she being my sister; to Priscella Fryer dau. of William Fryer after the decease of my wife Rose; to Daniel Jackson; to William son of John Fryer; Frances and Rose daus. of William Fryer; George and Elizabeth children of Daniel Jackson; Katherine dau. of John Fryer; exors. Thomas Robinson and William Fryer.

MARCEY, EDWARD, 28 May 1724; 30 Sept. 1724.

Sons John, Edward and Thomas; dau. Ann Marcy; wife Martha extx.

BERNARD, ROBERT, 4 Dec. 1724; 27 Jan. 1724.

To George Pierce and his son John; to George son of George Pierce; to Eliza. Manning; to Stephen Latharam; to Edward Riley; to Doctor Cooper; exors. my wife and George Pierce.

DOWLING, JAMES, 16 Mch. 1724; 26 May 1725.

Daughter Mary Dowling and wife Joanna.

FRANK, SARA, widow of Robert, ————; 20 June 1725.

Eldest son Thomas; sons Robert and Samuel; children Martha and Nehemiah; John Piper and wife Mary.

SMITH, CALEB, 15 June 1725; 28 July 1725.
Eldest son John; son Caleb; my five children; wife Elizabeth and brother John Smith exors.

MORRIS, ABRAHAM, 22 July 1725; 25 July 1725.
To Mary Harvey; wife Margarte and my son and daughter; exor. friend James Hord.

SMITH, JOHN, ———; 25 Aug. 1725.
Sons Thomas and John; wife Mary.

HOPWOOD, RICHARD, 15 Jan. 1725; 23 Feb. 1725.
Wife Mary; son Moses; son in law John Borrer; to Henry Borrer.

PEACH (or Peack), GEORGE, 6 Nov. 1717; 25 Feb. 1725.
Son Thomas; dau. Mary.

BROWN, JOHN, 26 Dec. 1725; 23 Feb. 1725.
Son Richard; son David when 18 years; dau. Sarah Brown; son William Brown's widow.

MASON, JOHN, 16 Jan. 1725; 23 Feb. 1725.
Cousin John Higdon when 20; to Richard Wroe; to William son of William Brown; to Mary Brown; to Hannah Wroe; to Walter Brown; to Original son of John Wroe; exors. Capt. Augustine Washington and William Brown.

MARTIN, MATTHEW, 22 Nov. 1725; 23 Feb. 1725.
Son Stephen; wife Hester; son Elias; granddau. Nannie Martin.

ROBINSON, JOHN, 8 Nov. 1725; 23 Feb. 1725.
Wife Mary; daus. Anne and Eliz. Robinson; exor. Brother Thos. Chancellor.

LOVELL, ROBERT, 15 Jan. 1725; 23 Feb. 1725.
Dau. Elizabeth Nicholson; dau. Mary Harrison; son Robert; sons Daniel and James; dau. Ursula Lovell; grandchildren Anne and Lovell Harris; exor. son Robert.

WROE, HENRY, 21 Nov. 1725; 23 Feb. 1725.
Sons Bunce and Henry Wroe; daughters Sarah, Elizabeth, Mary and Susanna Wroe; to Robert Stephens and Wife Elizabeth; wife Mary; brother Bunce Wroe exor.

SPURLING, JEREMIAH, 13 Feb. 1725; 30 Mch. 1726.
Wife Mary; eldest son Jeremiah; dau. Sarah Spurling; son Thomas; son John Banwell.

GLASCO, JOHN, 28 Jan. 1725-6; 30 Mch. 1726.
To John Chalker; to James Courtwell; to Gerrard Ball.

STEPHENS, ROBERT, 17 Feb. 1725-6; 30 Mch. 1726.
Godson Henry Wroe; godson James Herney; to Mary Wroe; to Elizabeth Gough she to be extx.

MUNROE, SPENCE, 15 Jan. 1725-6; 31 Mch. 1726.
My wife; brother Andrew Munroe; the child my wife goes with; my three children; exor. brother Andrew.

ELLIOTT, WILLIAM, 18 Mch. 1725-6; 27 Apl. 1726.
Wife Mary, to godson and nephew William Elliott; son in law Benj. Weeks.

CHANLOR, THOMAS, 11 May 1721; 29 June 1726.
Youngest son Francis the land bought of Walter English; sons Joseph and John; grandson Thomas Spurling; exors. friends Col. Thos. Lee and Capt. Henry Lee.

SANDERS, WILLIAM, 31 Mch. 1726; 29 June 1726.
Sons John, Phillip, William and James; wife Elizabeth; daughters Mary, Ursula, Elizabeth and Sarah Sanders.

PURSLEE, PATRICK, 5 Apl 1726; 29 June 1726.
Wife Ursula; dau. Ann Purslee; sons John, Thomas and James; brother Osman Jenkins; brothers John and Gerrard Bricke.

MUSE, ANN, 14 June 1725; 29 June 1726.
To son Edward land of my decd. husband; son William; son Hopkins; sons John, Augustine and George; dau. Mary Sanford bed now in possession of Thomas Muse, Jr.; dau. Ann Muse; son in law Robert Sanford; friend Benjamin Waddey.

BURN, JAMES, 12 Sept. 1724; 27 July 1726.
Wife Alice; sons William and James; grandson Daniel Burn.

BLAGG, MARGARET, 18 May 1724; 27 July 1726.
Grandson Abraham Blagg when 18; James Hore his uncle to advise him.

MINOR, WILLIAM, of Cople, 30 Jan. 1725; 28 Sept. 1726.
Sons John, William and Nicholas; daughters Mary, Jemima and Barbara Minor; wife Eliza; brother Nicholas Minor exor.

CHILTON, JOHN, 7 Aug. 1726; 28 Sept. 1726.
Son John land in Stafford; son Thomas; when Richard and John Watts come of age.

SORRELL, THOMAS, of Cople, 12 Jan. 1725; 22 Feb. 1726.
Son James; to son John land devised me by my father in law Daniel Occany; son James land in James City co., bequeathed me by my father John Sorrell, decd.; nephew Thomas Sorrell; my brother John decd.; aforesaid nephew and his sisters Elizabeth and Frances; daus. Anna and Winifred; wife Elizabeth; friends Capt. George Turberville and Mr. William Sturman.

BONAM, SAMUEL, St. Stephens Par. Northumberland, 6 Dec. 1726; 22 Feb. 1726.
Son Samuel; my brother Daniel Bonam; to Samuel son of George Haydon; my sister in law Mary Ball; wife Elizabeth and the child she goes with; my children to the care of my uncle George Eskridge till of age.

KING, JOHN, of Cople, 3 Dec. 1726; 22 Feb. 1726.
Son James; grandson John Spence; my brother's dau. Mary; son in law John Spence; wife Margaret; to Daniel son of Major George Eskridge.

MORRIS, ELIAS, 10 Aug. 1726; 22 Feb. 1726.
Wife Bridget; grandchildren Jeremiah and Elizabeth Nash; to countryman David Williams; exors. my wife and Nathaniel Nash.

WATTS, alias WATKINS, YOUELL, 8 Nov. 1726; 22 Feb. 1726.
Sister in law Hannah Broags; coz. Patrick Spence; to Wharton Ransdell; my wife; to Youell Hollam and his brother Simon.

BROWNING, THOMAS, 31 Jan. 1726; 22 Feb. 1726.
Dau. Jane wife of Andrew Hutchinson; dau. Ann widow of Morgan Williams; dau. Mary wife of Richard Omohundro.

BONUM, PHILPOT, 23 Nov. 1726; 22 Feb. 1726.
Brother Daniel Bonum; wife Rose; brother Samuel; to Richard Partridge; to James Thomas and James Thomas, Jr.

FRANK, ROBERT, 17 Nov. 1725; 22 Feb. 1726.
Granddau. Margaret Spilman; grandson Robert Frank; grandson William Plunkett; grandson John Grinning; granddau. Elizabeth Knighton; grandson Thomas Grinning; grandson Thomas Frank; exor. John Plunkett.

DUNKIN, JOHN, 20 June 1716; 22 Feb. 1726.
Son Peter land left by my decd. father Peter Dunkin; son William; daus. Elizabeth Ann and Alice; grandsons John and William Rochester; dau. Phillis Rochester; grandchildren John and Elizabeth children of James Dunkin; sons Peter, William and James; grandson John son of Peter.

AWBREY, JOHN, 19 Dec. 1726; 22 Feb. 1726.
Dau. Hannah Awbrey; dau. Keziah Attwell; dau. Kerrenhappuck Awbrey; son Chandler Awbrey.

WALKER, THOMAS, 11 Dec. 1726; 23 Feb. 1726.
Sons James, Thomas, Samuel, William and Hardidge; dau. Hannah land in Stafford; wife Lydia; exor. brother George Walker.

HARDWICH, JOSEPH, 24 Dec. 1726; 29 Mch. 1727.
Wife Ann and all my children when 16; exors. wife and nephew James Hardwich.

HAMBLETON, JAMES, 17 Nov. 1726; 29 Mch. 1727.
Wife Grace and my three children; sons James and John.

HAMBLETON, GRACE, 11 Feb. 1726-7; 29 Mch. 1727.
My decd. husband James; children James, John and Ann.

CARR, SARAH, widow of William Carr, 21 Nov. 1726; 29 Mch. 1727.
Daughters Elizabeth Bailey and Anne Carr.

LAMKIN, GEORGE, 21 Apl. 1718; 29 Mch. 1727.
Dau. Elenor Lamkin; sons Peter and George; wife Jean; brother James Lamkin exor.

DISHMAN, SAMUEL, 15 Nov. 1726; 31 May 1727.
Eldest son John land in Stafford; dau. Elizabeth Brown; dau. Ann; son James land in King George; son David; son Peter land in Essex; dau. Mary; wife Cornelia.

RUST, JOHN, 11 Apl. 1727; 31 May 1727.
Sons Samuel and John; to sons John and William land in Stafford and King George; dau. Elizabeth Rust; brother Jeremiah Rush exor.

RUSSELL, ANDREW, 13 Apl. 1727; 31 May 1727.
Children Francis and Anthony; wife Penelope.

REMY, JACOB, 23 Feb. 1726-7; 31 May 1727.
Sons John, Jacob, William, Benjamin and Joseph; my wife.

LONGWORTH, JOHN, 22 June 1724; 1 June 1727.
John Cockerell my son in law and William Sanders exors; children Anna, Frances, Margaret, Thomas and Elizabeth Longworth.

BRISCO, JAMES, 5 May 1727; 26 July 1727.
Dau. Elizabeth Butler; wife Margaret; son John; dau. Elenor; son James; my wife and her brother Henry Ward exors.

FRYER, JOHN, 22 Apl. 1727; 26 July 1727.
Wife Sarah; sons William and John.

MEACHAM, WILLIAM, 3 Jan. 1726-7; 26 July 1727.
To Daniel Jennings, John Morphew and Mary White; to brothers Richard, Samuel and Benjamin all lands in Gloucester county; to Youell Attwell.

NEWTON (Capt.), THOMAS, 26 Aug. 1727; 31 Jan. 1727.
Son Willoughby land in Richmond co.; dau. Elizabeth Wauhopes; grandson Nicholas Keene; son Rev. Walter Jones and Behethland his wife; wife Elizabeth; son Willoughby exor.

HALES, JOHN, 29 Jan. 1727; 31 July 1728.
Son George; dau. Mary King; grandson William Brown land in Stafford.

HARTLEY, JOHN, 12 Dec. 1726; 16 Apl. 1728.
Three children John, William and Sarah; wife Mary.

MARTIN, JACOB, 9 Jan. 1727-8; 30 Oct. 1728.
Dau. Sarah, dau. Ann Lovell; dau. Jane; wife Sarah; son John.

MOSS RICHARD, 2 Jan. 1728; 22 Jan. 1728.
Three children Frances, Thomas and Judith; brother John Moss exor.

BARNES, THOMAS, 28 Nov. 1728; 29 Jan. 1728.
Wife Ann; my three children Abraham, Elizabeth and Francis; brothers Abraham and Richard Barnes.

BRISCOE, MARGARET, 27 Nov. 1728; 29 May 1729.
Dau. Butler; dau. Ellenor; son James; exors. John Butler and John Briscoe.

CHANLOR, WILLIAM, 29 Jan. 1728; 31 July 1729.
To Eliz. Cooper my former wife's sister; to grandson Chanlor Awbury; to Susannah Applegate my present wife.

BERRYMAN, BENJAMIN, 4 Aug. 1729; 27 Aug. 1729.
Sons James, William, Maximilian, Newton, Henry and Benjamin; grandson Gilson Berryman; daughters Elizabeth, Rose, Ann, Sarah, Frankey and Kate; my wife.

BUTLER, CHRISTOPHER, 2 Oct. 1729; 26 Nov. 1729.
Son Nathaniel; brother Lawrence Butler; sons William, Lawrence, Joseph and John; my wife; son Caleb.

COOPER, ELIZA, 9 Jan. 1729-30; 25 Feb. 1729.
Daughter Marie Taylor; son William Walker; grandson George Mullins; son Spencer Watts.

RUST, MARTHA, 3 Nov. 1726; 25 Feb. 1729.
Dau. Hannah Eskridge; dau. Ann Harrison; son Peter Butler exor.; son Matthew Rust guardian of my son Peter Rust.

MELVIN, WILLIAM, 26 Apl. 1726; 25 Feb. 1729.
Son in law John Jennings; wife Elizabeth.

CARPENTER, ANN, 3 Feb. 1728; 25 Feb. 1729.
Son William; dau. Mary wife of John Halliday and their son Mathew.

ARISS, JOHN, 13 Mch. 1729; 25 Mch. 1730.
Son Spencer Ariss, son John, daus. Elizabeth and Frances Ariss.

KEATING, PIERCE, 13 Nov. 1729; 23 Mch. 1730.
Son James; dau. Malinda Keating.

MIDDLETON, BENEDICT, 31 Dec. 1729; 25 Mch. 1730.
Sons Robert, Benedict and William; daus. Mary, Elizabeth and Jane Middleton.

BROWN, DAVID, 8 July 1727; 26 Aug. 1730.
Grandson Original Brown; dau. Mary Bowling; sons Original, John and William.

WROE, WILLIAM, 8 Feb. 1725-6; 30 Sept. 1730.
Wife Hannah; sons Original, William and Richard; daus. Mary, Eliza, Sarah and Judith; to Margaret Anderson.

BENNETT, JOHN, 21 Jan. 1729-30; 28 Oct. 1730.
Wife Esther; dau. Elizabeth Summers.

HARGIS, JOHN, 19 June, 1730; 25 Nov. 1730.
Son John; dau. Mary Hargis; dau. Milvetto Hargis; brothers Roger Hargis and James Woring exors.

BINCKS, JOHN, 2 Feb. 1728; 24 Feb. 1730.
Sister Ann Green; to brother Thomas Bincks' children Mary and John; wife Elizabeth.

MOTHERSHEAD, JOHN, 13 Nov. 1730; 26 May 1731.
Sons Nathaniel, George, Christopher and John; dau. Elizabeth Quisenberry; dau. Ann Claytor; son Alvin; son George; grandson Brooks Mothershead; wife Elizabeth.

RUST, JEREMIAH, 7 Aug. 1731; 29 Sept. 1731.
Brother Peter; son Samuel land in Northumberland; son William; wife Magdalene; son Jeremiah; daus. Hannah and Martha Rust; child my wife goes with.

ROBINSON, WILLIAM, 26 June 1731; 27 Oct. 1731.
Son William when of age; daus. Ann and Elizabeth; my wife; exors. brother Michael Robinson and James Smith.

PEYTON, GERRARD, 27 Dec. 1687-8; 11 Jan. 1687-8.
To sister Elizabeth Hardidge all estate; father in law Mr. William Hardidge exor.
(NOTE. This will is recorded in Book 8., page 486. The page in the original book in which it was recorded has been lost.)

ASHTON, HENRY, 26 Feb. 1730; 24 Nov. 1731.
My wife; dau. Grace Ashton; my two granddaughters Elizabeth and Ann Aylett the daus. of Capt. William Aylett and Ann his wife who was my daughter, decd.; granddau. Elizabeth Turberville; son Henry; son John; dau. Elizabeth Ashton; cousin Burdett Ashton; to godson John son of Mr. Charles Ashton, decd.; sister Mrs. Sarah Macgill; exors. in trust Capt. George Turberville, Capt. Burdett Ashton, Mr. Andrew Monroe and Mr. Richard Watts.

HENRY, ROWLAND, ———; 26 Apl. 1732.
Dau. Hannah Henry; wife Mary extx.

McCARTY, ANN, 7 Nov. 1728; 31 May 1732.
To each of my own brothers and their wives a ring, also to Col. John Tayloe; son Henry Fitzhugh my first wedding ring and my grandfather Corbin's mourning ring; to Elizabeth Fitzhugh dau. of Major John Fitzhugh; dau. Lettice; dau. Sarah Fitzhugh; to Billington McCarthy my last wedding ring; to Thaddeus McCarthy; to Sarah Beale; I discharge my brothers Henry Fitzhugh and Thomas Fitzhugh and Henry Lee from the bills of exchange to my late husband McCarthy.

MUSE, THOMAS, 12 Mch. 1729; 28 June 1732.
My wife Elizabeth; sons Christopher, Daniel, James, Nicholas, John, and Thomas; dau. Ann Taylor; dau. Mary Muse; dau. Eliza Newman; granddau. Mary George.

STURMAN, WILLIAM, 15 June 1732; 27 Sept. 1732.
Son Foxhall; dau. Martha Sturman; wife Sarah; my four children.

HARDWICK, GEORGE, 30 June 1732; 27 Sept. 1732.
Brother James and his son William; my mother Elizabeth Hardwick.

MORTON, RICHARD, 18 Nov. 1731; 27 Sept. 1732.
Wife Massey and my children; exor. father in law Robert Sanford, Sr.

BAYLEY, ANN, 13 Mch. 1731-2; 25 Oct. 1732.
Granddaughter Ann Quisenberry, great grandson Banam Burch; granddau. Elizabeth Cox; great-grandson Bayley Washington; to Jane wife of Giles Esther; to Benj. Akers; to William Brown; granddaughter Mary Washington and her husband Henry Washington.

BLUNDALL, THOMAS, 8 Oct. 1731; 25 Oct. 1732.
Dau. Susanna Holladay; sons Thomas, Absolam, William and Garner; dau. Eliza McKenna; dau. Jane Blundall; son in law Richard Holladay and son in law William McKenna exors.

BONUM, DANIEL, 15 Oct. 1732; 28 Nov. 1732.
Son Samuel; nephews Thomas and Samuel Bonum; wife Sarah.

McKENNE, WILLIAM, 3 Nov. 1729; 28 Nov. 1732.
We William and Jane McKenne of Nominy being sick make this our will. Lands to our three sons Gerrard, John and Daniel; to son William; to grandchild Kenne Williams; to three daughters Deborah Marmaduke, Jane Williams and Mary Williams.

BUCKLEY, JOHN, 7 Mch. 1730; 30 Jan. 1732.
Wife Elizabeth and all my children; sons John, Abraham and William.

BUTLER, LAWRENCE (Capt.), 9 Mch. 1732; 27 Mch. 1733.
Dau. in law Corderoy Sanford; grandson William Bernard; niece Joyce Butler; son in law Richard Berbard; nephew Lawrence Butler; son Lawrence; dau. Sarah; to John Silvey; friend Capt. Anthony Thornton and Richard Bernard exors.

MIDDLETON, 9 Feb. 1732; 27 Mch. 1733.
Daughters Mary and Alice Middleton; grandson John Middleton; sons Benjamin, Thomas and Robert.

WIGGINTON, FRANCIS, 24 Dec. 1732; 27 Mch. 1733.
Cousin Elizabeth Cannady; Ann Bannister; godson Thomas Martin; dau. Elizabeth Wright; son in law Richard Wright; my husband and childrens' graves.

GOLORTHUM, MARTIN, 20 Nov. 1732; 27 Mch. 1733.
Sons John and William; Christ. Pritchett; wife Mary and five children.

FIELD,·DANIEL, 2 Feb. 1732-3; 28 Mch. 1733.
To Margaret Gerviss; to Mary Beckwith dau. of Alice Beckwith land in Prince William; to Daniel Hutson; wife Mary.

RICE, WILLIAM, ———; 17 May 1733.
Wife Mary; sons William, Nerobabel and John.

PATEN, ANTHONY, 23 Feb. 1731-2; 29 May 1733.
Son William; dau. Sarah Paten; sons John and Anthony; dau. Margaret Jett; son Samuel; dau. Mary Paten; son in law Francis Jett.

WALKER, WILLIAM, ———; 26 June 1733.
Sons William and Daniel; wife Ann; sons John, Richard and Joseph; dau. Martha Walker.

SELF, JOHN, 10 Dec. 1732; 26 June 1733.
Wife Susannah; sons John, Thomas, Moses and William; dau. Mary Self.

PIERCE, WILLIAM, 1 Aug. 1733; 25 Sept. 1733.
Sons William and Joseph; daughters Sarah, Mary, Elizabeth and Margaret Pierce; brother Robert Tomlin and Thomas Dozier exors.

TANNER, MARTHA, 7 Jan. 1733; 26 Feb. 1733.
To Richard Griffin and his son Lewis all my estate.

CREED, JAMES, 16 Oct. 1733; 26 Feb. 1733.
Son James; wife Elizabeth and my four children.

BUTLER, WILLIAM, 18 Jan. 1733-4; 26 Mch. 1734.
Son Cradock; son Gerard; my five children Cradock, Gerrard, Elizabeth, Sarah and Hannah Butler; dau. Jane Jeffries; brother Thomas Butler and Jeremiah Garland exors.

LINTON, WILLIAM, 6 Feb. 1733; 26 Mch. 1734.
Wife Mary; sons Anthony, William and John; dau. Elizabeth Lewis; cousin James Smith.

WILLIAMS, EDWARD, 26 Jan. 1733-4; 28 May 1734.
Brother William Williams; niece Elizabeth dau. of Joshua Williams; wife Sarah; niece Sarah dau. of William Williams; niece Frances dau. of Richard Haselrig.

HARNESS, WILLIAM, 25 Feb. 1733-4; 30 July 1734.
To Thomas Jenkins; son John; wife Martha and her son John Jenkins.

HARDWICK, ELIZABETH, 12 Aug. 1734; 29 Oct. 1734.
Grandchildren Barbara Walker, Rachel Walker and Frances Hardwick; to Hannah Awbrey and niece Hannah Hardwick; niece Anne Hardwick; son James Hardwick.

POPE, HUMPHREY, 10 Jan. 1732; 29 Oct. 1734.
Daughter Ann Conditt; dau. Sophia Muse; son Humphrey; son John; dau. Sarah Pope; dau. Mary Muse; dau. Mary Pope; to my wife's dau. Elizabeth Morrison; wife Mary and four youngest children; wife coz. Daniel McCarty and Peter Jett exors.

WEEDON, GEORGE, 23 May 1734; 26 Nov. 1734.
To John Pierce; my wife; Nathl. Gray, Jr. and Robert Lovell exors.

MUSE, THOMAS, 29 Oct. 1734; 26 Nov. 1734.
Brothers Christopher and Daniel; friend Benj. Waddey; son Thomas; my father in law Richard Sanford; brother in law Richard Sanford, Jr.; brother John Muse.

LOVELL, DANIEL, 9 Aug. 1733; 28 Jan. 1734.
Brothers Robert and James; sister Ursual Lovell.

HARRISON, GEORGE, 7 Feb. 1725-6; 28 Jan. 1734.
Sons George, Benjamin and Jeremiah; wife Ann; son Samuel.

COOPER, JOHN, 12 Oct. 1734; 25 Mch. 1735.
Wife Hannah; dau. Katherine Chancellor; grandson John Chancellor; son in law Thomas Chancellor.

MUSE, ELIZABETH, 29 Mch. 1735; 27 May 1735.
Sons William, Nicholas and Daniel; dau. Ann Chilton; dau. Elizabeth Barnet; to Barbara Minor; granddau. Mary Minor.

MORE, JOHN, 4 Jan. 1733-4; 25 Nov. 1735.
Son William; to Alice Garland; to Jeremiah Garland.

MOXLEY, JOSEPH, 18 May 1734; 30 Sept. 1735.
Sons Joseph and Christopher; brother Daniel; dau. Sarah Moxley; my wife; brothers John and Samuel.

ESKRIDGE, GEORGE (Colonel), 27 Oct. 1735; Nov. 1735.
Sons Samuel and William; dau. Elizabeth; the four sons of my son George decd.; son in law Willoughby Newton and Sarah his wife; dau. Margaret Kenner; son Robert; my wife.

VAUGHAN, CORDEROY, 13 July 1735; 25 Nov. 1735.
To Daniel Vaughan; to Anne Merman; to Peter Vaughan; wife Elenor and her dau. Ann Hays.

COLLINGSWORTH, THOMAS, 26 Nov. 1734; 25 Nov. 1735.
Sons Thomas, John and Willoughby; daughters Ann and Sarah Collingsworth.

FINCH, JOHN, 25 Dec. 1735; 27 Jan. 1735.
Daughter Mary Finch; sons Thomas, Richard and Blagdon.

BAILEY, JOHN, 11 June 1729; 30 June 1736.
Sons James and Stephen; son in law Edward Young.
SMITH, JOHN, 9 Dec. 1735; 27 Apl. 1736.
Sister Margaret Watson; wife Mary; son John.

COLEMAN, JAMES, 28 Dec. 1735; 27 Apl. 1736.
Godson Samuel son of Peter Rust; brother Richard Coleman.

JEFFRIES, EDMUND, 4 Dec. 1735; 25 May 1736.
Wife Ann; sons Jeremiah, Robert, George and Edmund; the children I have by my wife viz: Elizabeth, Ann, Mary, Catherine, Ellenor, Alice, Jeremiah and Robert; dau. Elizabeth Garner.

BULGER, EDMUND, 29 May 1736; 29 June 1736.
Daughter Mary; sons John and Edmund.

LEWIS, SURLES, 27 Dec. 1729; 29 June 1736.
Sons Thomas, Surles, John and James; dau. Sara Render; wife Elizabeth.

SHAW, WILLIAM, 7 June 1736; 29 June 1736.
To Elizabeth Sturman; Edward Ransdell, Jr.; Joseph Stone; sisters Sara and Jane Shaw.

MUSE, CHRISTOPHER, 18 Jan. 1734; 29 June 1736.
Brother Nicholas Muse and his son Nicholas; my uncle John Muse; land purchased by my father in 1718; cousin Thomas son of my decd. brother Thomas Muse

STEEL, JOHN, 16 Mch. 1735-6; 28 July 1736.
Son John; to Sarah Steel; son Richard; dau. Margaret Steel; son Thomas; daughters Mary and Elizabeth Steel; son Charles; wife Margaret.

BLUNDALL, WILLIAM, 21 July 1736; 30 Aug. 1736.
To Richard Holliday and wife Susannah all estate.

KENDALL, JOHN, 2 Sept. 1736; 22 Feb. 1736.
Estate to Mary Brock of King George.

TAYLOR, THOMAS, 8 Feb. 1735-6; Feb. 1736.
Wife Mary; sons Thomas, William, John and Richard; dau. Elizabeth wife of Amos Bagwell; grandchild Jane Bagwell.

CHILTON, MARY, 3 April 1737; 26 Apl. 1737.
Granddaughter Elizabeth Sanford; Capt. Andrew Monroe and his wife Jane; to John Watts; son James Bowcock and his children Thomas, James and Jane; sons Richard and John Watts; dau. Jane Monroe; daus. Margaret Strother and Mary Blackburn and the latter's husband Mr. Richard Blackburn; Rev. Roderick McCulloch; Capt. Thomas Chilton and wife Jemima.

MONROE, WILLIAM, 30 Mch. 1737; 26 Apl. 1737.
Son Thomas; grandson Thomas Monroe; grandson Spence and his brother Andrew Monroe; granddaughter Jane Monroe; son George; grandson George son of William Monroe; Jeane Payne; grandson Daniel Payne; dau. Sarah Stone; dau. Mary Stone; grandson William Payne; grandson Wm. Stone; son William Monroe; son Andrew Monroe's children Spence, Andrew and Jean; son William exor.

SANFORD, ROBERT, 3 June 1736; ——— 1737.
Sons Robert, John and Joseph; daughters Margaret Neale; Jemimah Minor; grandson Joshua Sanford; daughters Ann and Elizabeth; son Robert and Presley Neale exors.

JAMES, FRANCIS, 15 Dec. 1736; 31 May 1737.
Daughter Mary Sharpe; sons Francis and John; daughters Margaret and Sarah James.

HUDSON, FIELD, ——— Sept. ———; 28 June 1737.
Brother Joshua; estate to wife Susanna.

DICKINSON, THOMAS, mariner, 10 July 1734; 28 June 1737.
To Behethland ———; sister Mary Dickinson.

WILLIAMS, JOHN, 13 Mch. 1736; 26 July 1737.
Son John; dau. Elizabeth Williams; wife Elizabeth; brother Thomas W.

BALL, GERRARD, 13 June 1737; 26 July 1737.
Aunt Mary Courtney; brother Benony Ball; brother Samuel Ball when 16; brother George Ball.

HARDWICK, JAMES, 8 June 1737; 27 Sept. 1737.
Son Aaron; son George; wife Haney Ritta Hardwick; son William; my decd. brother George Hardwick; to William Garland, Jr., brother of my wife; dau. Frances Hardwick.

STURMAN, THOMAS, 1 April 1737; 30 Nov. 1737.
Son Thomas; son Richard; son William; son Valentine; to Mary Barker; dau. Ann Walker; granddau. Elizabeth Stuart; dau. Dorcas Raffedy; dau. Jemima.

WELLINGTON, JOHN, 29 Oct. 1737; 30 Nov. 1737.
Sara and Winifred Gobbs to stay with my wife Elizabeth until they arrive at 18 years; to coz. Michael Robinson; to Elizabeth McCarney.

CURTIS, THOMAS, 12 Oct. 1737; 30 Nov. 1737.
Wife Honor; son John; son Robert; dau. Mary Curtis.

MOOR, WILLIAM, 28 June 1736; 30 Jan. 1737.
Daughter Jane Creswick; son William; dau. Elizabeth; wife Alice and the rest of my children.

LAMKIN, JOHN, 15 Nov. 1737; 31 Jan. 1737.
Daughter Jane Moor; daughter Winifred Howell; to George Duren.

TYLER, JOSEPH, 3 Dec. 1737; 31 Jan. 1737.
Brother Benjamin Tyler; sister Christian Monroe; coz. Elinor Monroe; coz. Spence Monroe; coz. Andrew Monroe; friend James Lovell; friend Anne Harrison; brother William Tyler.

REMY, WILLIAM, aged 65; 19 Nov. 1737; 30 May 1738.
Son William; to Jacob Remy's heirs; to Aubrey Remy; dau. Mary Saunders; to Catherine Wormoth; sons John, James and Daniel; wife Catherine; to Elizabeth Sanders when she marries.

CHAPMAN, JOHN, master of the brigantine "Hopewell," 15 Sept. 1737; 27 June 1738.
To my brother Charles; my friend George Turberville, gent.

SANFORD, ROBERT, 23 March 1737; 29 Aug. 1738.
Son Augustine; son Joshua; my mother Mary Sanford now living; son Robert; my six daughters; daus. Elizabeth and Mary; exors. Edward Muse and Presley Neale.

HOWELL, JOHN, ———; ——— Aug. 1738.
Daughter Martha Attwell; wife Winifred; son John at 21; exor. Major George Turberville.

BOOK IX.

CRABB, DANIEL, 1 Dec. 1738; 30 Jan. 1738.
Brother Thomas when 21; brother John; brother Osman; sister Lettice Mc-Kenney; my mother Sarah Dunbar.

PARY, WILLIAM, stricken in years; 11 Feb. 1731-2; 31 Jan. 1738.
Wife Ann; grandson Franklin Pary; dau. in law Susanna Pary; son John Pary; granddaughters Ann and Caty.

POPHAM, JOHN, 31 Oct. 1738; 27 Mch. 1739.
Son Job; my three daus. Sophia, Mary and Ann; wife Rachel.

FREEID, WINIFRED, 6 Jan. 1738-9; 27 Mch. 1739.
To George Durwin when 17 years; to Jane Moore.

COOPER, HANNAH, 26 Dec. 1738; 29 May 1739.
Bushrod Thomas when 21; to William Sanford son of my sister Eliz. Sanford; my dau. Elizabeth Meriwether; dau. Sarah Berryman; son John Bushrod; dau. Hannah Neale; my late husband Col. Willoughby Allerton who gave his bond for my dau. Hannah Neale, by name of Hannah Bushrod; (Note: This name is written both Neale and Heale in the body of the will); son in law William Fauntleroy; dau. Apphia Fauntleroy; son Richard Bushrod the land I bought of John Jewell and Elizabeth his wife; I desire my son Richard Bushrod to bury me between his father Richard Bushrod and Mr. Cooper; son Richard exor.

ROWBOTHAM, ELIZABETH, 11 July 1739; 31 July 1739.
To Mary Payne all estate.

ALLERTON, ISAAC, 31 Mch. 1739; 27 Nov. 1739.
Wife Ann; three sons Gawin, Willoughby and Isaac; sister Elizabeth Quill's children Sarah and Margaret; coz. Charles Beale and his brothers John, Taverner, Richard and Reuben; wife Ann and friend John Bushrod and Daniel Hornby exors.

HIGDON, DANIEL, 26 Oct. 1739; 27 Nov. 1739.
My daughters Mary and Jane; son in law John Muse; wife Margaret; to Humphrey Pope that married my daughter in law Sarah; to John McLarran.

TYNON, WILLIAM, 21 Aug. 1737; 27 Nov. 1739.
To John Booth; to Ellenor Garner; to James Grase; to Mary Ann Garner; to Rebecca Eskridge; Joseph Garner and John Booth exors.

JETT, MARGARET, 26 Sept. 1739; 27 Nov. 1739.
To granddau. Elizabeth Morris; granddaughter Margaret Morris; Mr. Daniel McCarthy, exor.

JETT, PETER, of King George Co., 27 Sept. 1728; 27 Nov. 1739.
To wife Margaret my whole estate.

DESHMAN, JOHN, 27 Mch. 1738; 27 Nov. 1739.
Wife Susannah; my four children Franklin, Ann, Kate and Roderick Perry; exors. friends Richard Sanford, Richard Sanford, Jr., and Robert Sanford.

FOOTMAN, JOHN, 19 Oct. 1739; 27 Nov. 1739.
To my wife Elizabeth; dau. Hannah Footman; kinsman John West of Northumberland Co.; to Footman Brown; friend Wharton Ransdell.

MONROE, SARAH, 25 July 1739; 27 Nov. 1739.
To son John Elliott; dau. Sibella Elliott; grandson John Elliott; grandson Foxhall Sturman; grandson Spence Monroe; to Mr. Wharton Ransdell; daughter Sarah Ransdell; my five grandchildren Elizabeth, Sarah, Martha Sturman, Thomas Ransdell and Sarah Elliott Ransdell; exor. John Elliott.

SPENCE, PATRICK, 10 Dec. 1739; 25 Mch. 1740.
To son Patrick; son Youell Spence the land given me by Youell Watts, decd.; wife Jemima; my four children Elizabeth, Jemima, Mary and Youell Spence; exors. my wife and son in law Nicholas Minor, Jr.

HUTT, GERRARD, 15 Nov. 1739; 25 Mch. 1740.
My sons Daniel, Gerrard and Thomas Hutt; wife Anne; my daughters Frances, Elizabeth, Susannah and Anne; grandson John Hutt; wife Anne and sons Gerrard and Thomas exors.

PEARSE, GEORGE, 27 Oct. 1739; 25 Mch. 1740.
To son John land in Stafford; son George; son William; dau. Margaret Pearse.

BEARD, JOHN, 10 Oct. 1739; 25 Mch. 1740.
Sons George and John; wife Ann extx.

BINKS, THOMAS, 1 Feb. 1739; 25 Mch. 1740.
Son John; dau. Mary Binks; sons Thomas and George and dau. Margt. Binks.

ASHTON, 6 Apl. 1739; 29 Apl. 1740.
My brother Burdett Ashton; to Richard Rallings his rent now due; brother Charles Ashton; coz. John eldest son of Charles Ashton; exors. brothers Charles and Burdett Ashton.

BRENAN, OWEN, ———; 27 May 1740.
To wife Deliverance; sons John and Owen; daughters Hannah and Ann.

ASBURY, HENRY, 27 Sept. 1739; 27 May 1740.
To sons Henry, William and Thomas; my wife Hannah; my children Sarah, George, Hannah, Isabella and Ann Asbury; exors. wife and son Henry.

WASHINGTON, LAWRENCE, 5 Feb. 1739; 24 June 1740.
To son John one-half my land, and sons James and Thomas the other half between them; to wife Elizabeth all movable estate and she to be extx.

DICKSON, ELIZABETH, 3 Nov. 1740; 25 Nov. 1740.
Son Francis Sharp; son Jeremiah Stephens; grandson James Stephens; son Burdett Stephens to be exor.

WEEDON, JOHN, Snr., 23 Sept. 1740; 25 Nov. 1740.
To son John; eldest son Augustine Weedon; eldest dau. Mary and youngest dau. Sarah; two sons to be exors.

SMITH, PETER, 10 Jan. 1738; 12 May 1741.
My dau. Mary Fleming; son Peter; son James the land in Prince William where he now lives; sons Thomas and William; dau. Abigail Fleming; granddau. Ann Bailey; dau. Anne Thomas; dau. Mary Fleming; dau. Hannah Ware; dau. Martha McClanahan; son Peter exor.

HEADLEY, ROBERT, ———; 12 June 1741.
Son William; son in law David Heale; granddaughters Mary Smith and Elizabeth Pickett; wife Mary extx.

SANFORD, JOSEPH, 3 April 1741; 26 April 1741.
Wife Mary; dau. Nanny; son Robert when 20; dau. Betty; Presley Neale to have the care of son Robert and dau. Nancy; Thomas Shaw to have the care of dau. Betty; brother John Sanford; son Robert to be bound to Thomas Sanford, Jr., bricklayer when 14.

MOTHERSHEAD, JOHN, ———; 17 June 1741.
My dau. Ann Quisenberry; dau. Elizabeth Mothershead; son Charles; my wife and three youngest children; sons William and John; daus. Sarah and Mary; wife Ann and son William exors.

STEELE, CHARLES, 7 Apl. 1741; 30 June 1741.
To brother Thomas Steele; sister Sarah Steele; my mother Margaret to be extx.

BUSH, EDWARD, 30 April 1741; 25 Aug. 1741.
To son Edward Francis Bush begot of my now wife Ann; to Frances Earls; exors. Thomas Finch and John Williams.

WRIGHT, RICHARD, 10 Mch. 1740; 27 Oct. 1741.
To godson William Davis; brother in law Gerrard Davis; sister Ann Davis; Brother John Wright; son Francis; dau. Elizabeth Wright; my wife Elizabeth.

WARD, HENRY, 15 Sept. 1741; 26 Jan. 1741.
My dau. Elizabeth Ward; dau. Sarah Ward; friends John Pownall and his wife Elizabeth to be guardians to my dau. Jane; my wife Mary.

RUST, WILLIAM, 6 Nov. 1741; 26 Jan. 1741.
To sons Samuel, William and Henry; daughter Mary Rust; my brother Peter Rust and my sister Ann Harrison.

CARR, JOSEPH, 12 Sept. 1741; 26 Jan. 1741.
To sons Joseph and James; daughter Mary Carr; to sister Ann Remy's son Joseph Remy.

POPE, THOMAS, 1 May 1741; 23 Feb. 1741.
My wife Mary and dau. Elizabeth; grandchildren of Samuel Hath.

TURBERVILLE, GEORGE, of Hickory Hill, 31 Dec. 1741; 30 Mch. 1742.
To dau. Elizabeth Turberville; late wife Frances dau. of Col. Henry Ashton mother of said Elizabeth; my wife Martha dau. of Mrs. Martha Lee, decd; dau. Lettice Turberville; son John; Col. Henry Lee, Landon Carter and my godson John Tayloe son of the Honl. John Tayloe of Richmond Co., to be exors; to John Hobson son and heir of John Hobson; the child my wife now goes with.

WILLIAMS, JOHN, 14 Jan. 1741-2; 13 Apl. 1742.
My wife Elizabeth and son Charles.

MELDRUM, MICHAEL, 13 Nov. 1741; 27 Apl. 1742.
My wife Mary; all the children of William Jenkins by his wife Mary.

YELLOP, THOMAS, tailor, 18 Jan. 1741; 25 May 1742.
Friend Nimrod Hutt of Prince William; friend William Cope; to Winifr...
and Sarah Gibbs; John son of John and Mary Murphy; brother Yellop of Co.
Suffolk in Gt. Britain and my sisters Mary and Ann.

BRUCE, GEORGE, 27 Jan. 1741-2; 29 June 1742.
To my sons William and George; to dau. Jane wife of Jacobus Jordan; dau.
Christian wife of John Young; son Charles; wife Margary; daus. Kezia and
Hannah Bruce.

BOWCOCK, JAMES, 12 Mch. 1741-2; 29 June 1742.
To my sons Thomas, James, John and Anthony; wife Sarah; dau. Jane.

MOORE, THOMAS, 17 Dec. 1741; 31 Aug. 1742.
To sons William and Thomas; daus. Sarah and Mary Moore.

SMITH, LAZARUS, 16 July 1742; 31 Aug. 1742.
Brother James Smith; to godson Spencer son of Thomas Smith, decd., when
he is 21; coz. Richard son of Richard Nutt and his wife Eliz.; goddau. Judith
dau. of William Smith; brother John Smith.

MURPHY, JOHN, 19 July 1742; 26 Oct. 1742.
Sons John and Samuel; dau. Elizabeth; wife Mary.

STONEHOUSE, ELIZABETH, 14 Apl. 1738; 1 Dec. 1742.
My two sons St. John Shropshire and Winfield Shropshire.

BALL, GEORGE, 15 Feb. 1742-3; 29 Mch. 1743.
my brother Emanuel Ball; brother Samuel Ball.

CHAMBERS, THOMAS, 7 Jan. 1742; 26 Apl. 1743.
To wife Mary all estate.

GRAY, NATHANIEL, 6 Mch. 1743; 26 Apl. 1743.
To son Nathaniel land in Stafford; son George; dau. Sarah Strother; grand-
son George Weedon; dau. Margaret Gray; son Francis; my wife; friend
William Strother exor.

BUTLER, CATHERINE, ——— Nov. 1730; 26 Apl. 1743.
To sons James and John; coz. Sarah Anderson; coz. Thomas Price; exors.
brothers William and James Butler.

THOMAS, JAMES, 1 Dec. 1742; 31 May 1743.
Sons James and George; dau. Winifred Thomas; dau. Elizabeth Thomas;
son John; grandson William Thomas son of dau. Katherine; dau. Hannah
Thomas; dau. Sarah Jenkins; wife Sarah.

STEEL, JOHN, 3 Oct. 1743; 29 Nov. 1743.
To Mary Steel alias Weeks dau. of Margaret Steel the plantation that Richard
Steel now lives on; to Thomas Steel; to Sarah Finch; exor. Benjamin Weeks.

47

BOOK X

MINOR, NICHOLAS, 11 Oct. 1743; 29 May 1744.
To son William Stewart Minor when 21; sons John and Nicholas; dau. Elizabeth; wife Jemima.

COX, CHARNOCK, 1 Mch. 1743; 26 June 1744.
To sons Presley, Charnock, Vincent and John; my wife.

AYLETT, WILLIAM, 29 Mch. 1744; 28 Aug. 1744.
My decd. father William Aylett of King William co., and my first wife's father Col. Henry Ashton, decd.; my two daughters Elizabeth and Anne issue of my first marriage, when they are 21; my wife Elizabeth and Anne and Mary her children; my brother John Aylett decd.; my brother Philip Aylett; brother Benjamin Aylett; Major Lawrence Washington; son in law Augustine Washington; brother Philip and Daniel McCarty exors.

FOOTMAN, ELIZABETH, 10 May 1744; 28 Aug. 1744.
My daughter Frances Youell; granddau. Elizabeth Youell; son in law Batteran Youell; William Rice, Snr.; my three children; my two sons Winder and Richard Kenner.

DEMOVEL, HANNAH, 8 Sept. 1744; 25 Sept. 1744.
To Peter son of George Lamkin decd.; my granddaughters Hannah Demovel, Mary Middleton and Hannah Armistead; Sarah dau. of John Armistead; my grandchildren Jane More, Hannah Brown, Magdalen Jackson, Hannah Hartley, James Lamkin, Samuel Lamkin and Magdalen Claughton; my dau. Elizabeth Middleton; son in law Benj. Middleton.

JARVIS, JOHN, 7 Mch. 1743-4; 30 Oct. 1744.
My sons John and Field; daughters Elenor, Catherine and Jane; my wife extx.

MOXLEY, WILLIAM, 8 May 1744; 30 Oct. 1744.
My son Daniel and his wife Mary; grandson Richard son of Richard Moxley; grandson William Payton; sons Samuel, William and Thomas; youngest son Daniel exor.

ESKRIDGE, ELIZABETH, 20 Oct. 1744; 27 Nov. 1744.
To Cradock Butler; my daughter Elizabeth Aylett; goddaughter Judith Newton; to Mary Luck; extx. dau. Elizabeth Aylett, widow.

FLEMING, JOHN, 15 Nov. 1744; 26 Feb. 1744.
James Bailey to be exor; son Peter; daughters Sarah and Anne; son Thomas; son William.

REYNOLDS, ROBERT, 11 Feb. 1744; 26 Feb. 1744.
My wife Nancy extx.; my children.

DODD, JOHN, 16 Sept. 1744; 26 Mch. 1745.
My sons Joseph, Nathaniel and Benjamin; daughter Mary McKenny and her husband John; daughter Elizabeth.

HAYES, HENRY, 14 June 1744; 26 Mch. 1745.
Son William when 21; wife Jane and all my children; William Garland, Jr., of Richmond co., exor.

RUST, MARTHA, 23 Dec. ——— ; 28 May 1745.
My brothers Samuel, Henry and William Rust; uncle Peter Rust exor.

GARNER, HENRY, 4 June 1744; 25 June 1745.
My wife Catherine; sons Thomas, Henry and Bradley Garner; daughter Hannah Allson; daughter Elizabeth Garner.

MOTHERSHEAD, CHRISTOPHER, 11 June 1745; 25 June 1745.
My son Christopher; wife Elenor and the child she goes with; dau. Sarah wife of John Pope; sister Anne Claytor; wife and Alven Claytor exors.

GRACE, JAMES, 26 Nov. 1744; 30 July 1745.
My wife Johannah and the child she goes with.

BASHAW, PETER, 9 Oct. 1745; 26 Nov. 1745.
My sons Peter, Warrener and James; to Spence Bashaw; daughters Elizabeth, Mary and Sarah Bashaw; wife Mary.

DANELEY, URSULA, 23 April 1745; 28 Jan. 1745-6.
Son Joseph Taylor exor.; daughter Mary Martin; son Philip Taylor.

FIELDER, ELIZABETH, 2 Dec. 1745; 25 Feb. 1745-6.
To daughter Jemima all estate.

McCULLOCK, RODERICK, 11 Nov. 1745; 25 Feb. 1746.
My son Roderick to be of age at 18; daughters Isabel and Elizabeth.

BLACKMORE, GEORGE, 10 Oct. 1745; 25 Feb. 1746.
To Lovel White the land bought of his father John White; to William son of my brother Samuel Blackmore of the parish of St. Mary Ottry, Co. of Devon in Gt. Britain; to coz. Samuel Blackmore son of my brother Samuel; to Gideon Blackmore my cozen son of Gideon Blackmore; my wife.

ROGERS, JOSEPH, 26 Jan. 1736; 25 March 1746.
To wife Mary all estate.

MOTHERSHEAD, WILLIAM, 1 May 1746; 27 May 1746.
To Charles Mothershead; brother John; to Sarah wife of Thomas James; John Mothershead and John Quisenberry exors.

CREED, JOHN, 27 Jan. 1745; 27 May 1746.
To Joseph son of William Weeks; to Jane dau. of Mary Brown; Robert Vaulx exor.

EARL, SAMUEL, 6 Aug. 1744; 29 July 1746.
My daughter Phillis Mockridge; daughters Hannah Baley and Elizabeth Hackney; grandson Samuel and John Earl; son Samuel Earl and Peter Rust exors.

RICHARDSON, JONATHAN, 17 Sept. 1746; 28 Oct. 1746.
To wife Elizabeth and all my children.

GREENWOOD, DANIEL, 25 Nov. 1746; 24 Feb. 1746-7.
William Welch to have my son Daniel until he is 21.

GRACE, FRANCES, 4 Oct. 1744; 24 Feb. 1747.
Son Henry Duncan; daughters Mary Scott and Elizabeth McBoyd.

GARRARD, WILLIAM, 4 Nov. 1746; 25 Feb. 1747.
My son Nathaniel; grandson William Garrard son of Nathaniel; to son Aaron Garrard; daughter Jane Garrard; daughter Sarah Garrard; wife Mary extx.; my four children.

REID, JOHN, son of George Reid in Middle-Heillar, parish of Dallgain, alias Sorn in the Shire of Ayr., 17 Jan. 1746; 31 Mch. 1747.
To my father George Reid all my estate; to Capt. John Aitken, commander of the snow, "Friendship," of Ayr, exor.

FORD, GERRARD, 10 Nov. 1746; 26 May 1747.
My sons Daniel and Warner; daughter Elizabeth Ford; wife Elizabeth.

LEE, HENRY, Parish of Cople, 28 Aug. 1747; 21 Oct. 1747.
My sons John and Richard; my father Col. Richard Lee decd.; son Henry; my grandfather Henry Corbin and his daughter Lettice who was my mother; my brother Richard Lee; daughter Lettice; wife Mary; brothers Thomas Lee, Esq., and Col. William Beverley and sons John and Richard exors. Codicil 15 Oct. 1747. My daughter Lettice wife of William Ball of Lancaster, gent.

LAMBERT, THOMAS, 1 Dec. 1747; 26 Jan. 1747-8.
My daughters Taker Smith and Elizabeth Stapleton; my sons William, Thomas and John; wife Rose; daughter Ann Lambert; son George.

SUTTON, RICHARD, 1 Oct. 1747; 23 Feb. 1747-8.
My sons Richard, James and Jacob; grandson William son of John and Elizabeth Sutton; daughter Mary Hazelrigg; wife Mary.

HERLEY, ELIZABETH, 30 Nov. 1747; 24 Feb. 1747-8.
My servant William Baxter; goddaughter Sarah Fisher; to Mrs. Ann Washington; to friend Augustine Washington my estate.

BOOK XI.

READ, COLEMAN, 1 Mch. 1747-8; 26 Apl. 1748.
My son Joseph; to ———; to son Richard after the death of my wife Ruth; daughters Mary and Susannah; grandchildren Coleman Brown, Coleman Dunkin, Ruth Asberry, Elizabeth Read and grandson Hutt.

COX, PETER, 12 Jan. 1747; 26 Apl. 1748.
My wife Mary; my five children Mary, Sarah, James, Peter and Hannah Cox; wife, Daniel Tebbs, George Lamkin and George Cox exors.

OLIFF, GEORGE, 3 Apl. 1748; 31 May 1748.
Sons George and James; daughter Rebecca; grandchildren Ann Oliff and Jemima Thrashall.

WIGGINTON, HENRY, 17 June 1748; 26 July 1748.
Uncle Roger Wigginton and his son Spencer; friend Mrs. Mary Lee; coz. Samuel son of Peter Rust; coz. Elizabeth dau. of Richard Wright; coz. Elizabeth wife of Dr. Thomas McFarlans; exors. George and Richard Lee.

MINOR. JOHN, 13 Sept. 1748; 25 Oct. 1748.
All my children; wife Mary and my father in law John Barnett and friend John Stowers exors.

BONUM, SAMUEL, 26 Oct. 1748; 29 Nov. 1748.
Uncle and Aunt Thomas and Elizabeth Bennett; cousins Mary, Thomas and Joseph Bennett; to Mrs. Sarah Newton; to Mrs. Elizabeth Newton; to Miss Judith Newton; to John Newton; to Capt. Willoughby Newton.

WILLIAMS, CHAMBERS, 12 Jan. 1748-9; 31 Jan. 1748-9.
Edward Guinness and wife Catherine; son Daniel at 18; son Thomas; to John Higdon and his wife Sarah; exor. Humphrey Pope.

BALEY, WILLIAM, 28 Aug. 1748; 31 Jan. 1748-9.
Granddaughter Ann Wood her aunt Mary Baley's wearing apparel; coz. James Baley; daughter Elizabeth Davis; nephew James Baley and his son William Baley.

DUNKIN, PETER, 13 Sept. 1748; 31 Jan. 1748-9.
Friend James Baley to have charge of my son until said son Charles is 21; son George.

SANDFORD, WILLIAM, 22 Jan. 1739-40; 28 Feb. 1748-9.
Daughter Martha Rhodes; son Joseph; dau. Frances Sanford; grandson John Ethel; son William.

BELL, THOMAS, 19 Aug. 1742; 25 April 1749.
To wife Johannah; sons Thomas and Joseph.

BAKER, JOHN, 3 Sept. 1748; 25 Apl. 1749.
Eldest son William; son John; dau. Anne Baker; daughters Frances and Mary Baker; wife Sarah; grandson Presley Baker.

HALCOM, GEORGE, ———; 27 June 1749.
My daughters Susanna, Mary, Milly, Jenny and Hannah Halcom; wife Isabel and Richard Padgett exors.

CRITCHER, JOHN, 27 Mch. 1749; 25 July 1749.
Sons John and Richard; daughter Anne McClave; dau. Mary Critcher; son Thomas; daughter Jean Critcher; daughter Eleanor Coleman.

GARNER, ARCHIBALD, 15 Apl. 1749; 29 Aug. 1749.
Children Jemima and Jane Joyce Garner at 18; friend Daniel Tebbs exor.

POPE, WORDEN, 14 Jan. 1748; 29 Aug. 1749.
To children Benjamin, Jean, William and the child my wife Hester goes with.

HARDWICK, JAMES, 12 June 1749; 31 Oct. 1749.
Sons Thomas and John; son in law Elias Davis; daughter Elizabeth Nash; daughter Sarah Summers; dau. ——— Lane; wife Elizabeth; son James.

JACKSON, CHRISTOPHER DOMINICK, 1 July 1749; 31 Oct. 1749.
Wife Magdalene and my three sons when they are 21.

51

KILL, CHARLES, 4 Jan. 1749; 30 Jan. 1749.
To Anne, Sarah and Francis Franklin they being the daughters of my sister Elizabeth Franklin, decd.; to Mary Franklin; wife Mary; son in law Benj. Weekes; Charles Weekes Steel son of Margaret Weekes.

DAVIS, ELIAS, 20 Dec. 1748; 30 Jan. 1749.
Son Youell; son Elias; dau. Amy Sutton; dau. Ann Packett; son John; wife Elizabeth, son Youell and Thomas Templeman exors.

HARRISON, WILLOUGHBY, 12 Jan. 1749-50; 27 March 1750.
Eldest son Samuel; son Joshua; son Daniel; dau. Dorcas Harrison; dau. Elizabeth Baley; son Willoughby.

MOTHERSHEAD, JOHN, 28 Nov. 1748; 27 Mch. 1750.
Daughter Mary Mothershead when of age; my brother Charles Mothershead when 21; wife Sarah and brother John Quisenberry exors.

BUTLER, ELIZABETH, 19 Jan. 1749; 27 March 1750.
Brother in law Thomas Butler; decd. husband William Butler; to Catherine Hardidge; my brother Presley Cockerill; to Elenor Clington; to Aunt Jane Wroe.

MOORE, THOMAS, 4 Feb. 1749-50; 24 Apl. 1750.
My sons Thomas and James; wife Winifred.

RALLINGS, SAMUEL, 17 Aug. 1749; 24 Apl. 1750.
Wife Martha; son Samuel; children Benjamin, Martha and Mary Rallings.

DAVIS, SAMUEL, 29 Oct. 1746; 29 May 1750.
Eldest son Joshua land in Prince William; youngest son Samuel land in Prince William; youngest dau. Esther Davis; eldest dau. Ann Davis; daughters Mary, Elizabeth, Frances and Catherine Davis; wife Ann.

CALLIS, WILLIAM, 5 Nov. 1747; 29 May 1750.
Sons John and Francis land in Prince William; sons Ambrose, Thomas, William, James and Richard; daughter Sarah; wife Sarah.

PARTRIDGE, RICHARD, 4 Apl. 1750; 29 May 1750.
Son Mathew; wife Jean and her sons Charles and Ashton Lamkin.

KENDALL, SAMUEL, 22 Jan. 1747; 31 July 1750.
Eldest dau. Sarah; daughters Ann, Martha and Mary; wife Sarah; daughters Gladys and Elizabeth; sons Moses and William; coz. John Kendall and John Macormack exors.

SMITH, JOSEPH, 29 Dec. 1749; 28 Aug. 1750.
Daughter Jemima Monroe; wife Sarah; to Augustine Goff; son Joseph; son Samuel; son Gideon.

ELLIOTT, AUGUSTINE, 11 June 1750; 28 Aug. 1750.
Mother Sibella Elliott extx. sisters Betty and Mildred Elliott; sister Martha Elliott.

HOLLAND, SIMON, 7 July 1750; 28 Aug. 1750.
Wife Esther; son Youell Holland; daughters Hannah and Elizabeth.

ROCHESTER, WILLIAM, 23 Oct. 1750; 30 Oct. 1750.
Son John; wife Frances and her son Daniel McKenny; son William.

WHITE, JOHN, aged 63; 18 Feb. 1747; 29 Jan. 1750-1.
Son George; dau. Mary; dau. Ann Walker; son William; dau. Sarah Russell; grandchildren John and Elizabeth White; wife Mary.

COX, CHARNOCK, 3 Mch. 1751; 26 Mch. 1751.
My sons Presley, George and William; dau. Elizabeth Rust; grandchildren Peter, Molly and Elizabeth Rust; son in law Samuel Rust.

COLLINSWORTH, THOMAS, 11 Dec. 1750; 26 Mch. 1751.
Sons John and Thomas; daughters Ann and Sarah Collinsworth; wife Ann and Willoughby Collinsworth exors.

MUSE, JOHN, 23 Jan. 1750; 26 Mch. 1751.
Daughter Susannah Muse; daughter Ann Muse; my three daughters; wife Margaret.

HALL, ANN, 15 Jan. 1750; 26 Mch. 1751.
To Ann Crumnil; Elizabeth Minor dau. of John Minor; to John Muse's two daughters Ann and Elizabeth; John Muse remainder of estate.

LEWIS, ELIZABETH, 6 Dec. 1750; 26 Mch. 1751.
Son John; son in law ———— Lewis; to John son of Catherine Garrard; to William Roussau and his brother James; son William Roussau exor.

MINOR, WILLIAM STEWART, ———— ; 26 Mch. 1751.
Wife Frances; dau. Frances when of age.

CRAWFORD, ROBERT, 6 Mch. 1750-1; 26 Mch. 1751.
Friend Daniel Tebbs; to Elizabeth Crabb; to Thomas Smith.

SANFORD, JOSEPH, 29 Dec. 1750; 30 Apl. 1751.
Wife Barbara; son Joseph; dau. Mary Sanford; child my wife now bears.

TAYLOR, JAMES, 23 Feb. 1750-1; 30 Apl. 1751.
My dau. Frances when 15; wife Sarah; friends George Franklin and Richard Payne exors.

WHITE, JOHN, 22 Sept. 1750; 30 Apl. 1751.
Eldest son Samuel; children John, Jenny and Susan White; wife Sarah extx.

ELLIOTT, SABELLAH, 8 Dec. 1750; 29 Jan. 1751.
My daughters Martha, Mildred and Betty Elliott; my decd. son Augustine Elliott; exor. Richard Barnes of Richmond co.

LEE, THOMAS, of Stafford, 22 Feb. 1749-50; 30 Apl. 1751.
My late dear wife and my honored mother decd.; to oldest son land in Westmoreland and Northumberland; my second, third, fourth and my other younger sons; daughter Alice; nephew George Lee; daughter Hannah Corbin; exors. Richard Corbin, my eldest son Philip Ludwell Lee, son in law Gawin Corbin and my second son Thomas Ludwell Lee.

RUST, MATHEW, 11 July 1751; 30 July 1751.
To Fleet Cox; son Vincent; son George; grandson Daniel Lamkin when 21 years; dau. Anne Lamkin; daughters Winifred and Sarah Rust; to wife Frances land bought of Samuel Rust; son Benedict; daughters Frances and Molly Rust; brother Peter Rust.

LAMKIN, SAMUEL, 28 Nov. 1751; 27 Aug. 1751.
To son Daniel estate when he is 21; my two brothers Ashton and Charles Lamkin.

LONGWORTH, BURGESS, 7 Nov. 1751; 26 Nov. 1751.
Son John; son in law Edward Pridham; dau. Ann Jordan; dau. Betty Thornton; dau. Frances Pridham; son William land in Richmond co.; son Burgess; dau. Mary.

PRICE, MEREDITH, 1 May 1749; 26 Nov. 1751.
Brother William Price; sister Martha Harrison.

DOZIER, RICHARD, 5 May 1739; 26 Nov. 1751.
Son in law Thomas Templeman; sons Richard, Thomas and William; grandson Dozier Templeman; dau. Margaret Templeman; dau. Elizabeth Wilson; to Daniel Muse; children Sarah Dozier, Hannah Muse, Martha and Mary Dozier and my granddaughter Elizabeth Bellfield; wife Elizabeth.

THOMPSON, JOHN, 24 Oct. 1751; 21 Nov. 1751.
Wife Elizabeth; son William when 20; George son of Richard Halliday; friend William Nicholls.

TEMPLEMAN, THOMAS, 25 May 1751; 25 Feb. 1752.
Daughter Mary Templeman; son Dozier; son William; son Richard Hodgson Templeman; son John; dau. Margaret Brewer; dau. Mary Templeman; son Dozier and brother in law Richard Dozier, Jr., exors.

SANFORD, THOMAS, 27 Sept. 1749; 25 Feb. 1752.
Sons Thomas, Robert and Richard; wife Dorcas.

MARSHALL, JOHN, 1 Apl. 1752.
Daughter Sarah Lovell negro in possession of Robert Lovell; dau. Ann Smith; dau. Elizabeth Smith; wife Elizabeth; sons Thomas, John and Abraham; daughters Margaret and Peggy Marshall.

ARROWSMITH, RICHARD, 5 Feb. 1752; 30 June 1752.
Son Thomas; grandsons William Arrowsmith and William Bittey; granddaughters Elizabeth Arrowsmith and Mary Bittey; wife Elizabeth.

POPE, JANE, 3 Apl. 1752; 30 June 1752.
My daughter Elizabeth Price; grandchildren Ann Price, William Price, Benjamin Pope and Elizabeth Pope; grandson John son of my dau. Elizabeth Price.

BUTLER, JAMES, 27 Jan. 1749; 28 July 1752.
Wife Ann; sons Thomas and James; grandson James Butler; dau. Mary Butler; Elizabeth Sanford; grandchildren James and Ann Kirk; grandchildren William and Sarah Jackson

GATHAGIN, JAMES, 17 Mch. 1752; 28 July 1752.
Wife Mary; dau. Mary Gathagin.

BOOK XII.

BAYLEY, STEPHEN, Snr., 14 Apl. 1750; 28 Aug. 1753.
Sons Stephen, John, William and James; daughters Ann Danielson, Martha Jenkins and Elizabeth ———; wife Elizabeth.

WILSON, ALLEN, 12 Aug. 1753; 27 Nov. 1753.
Sister Hannah Borer; exor. Henry Borer.

KENDALL, JOHN, 30 Jan. 1754; 26 Mch. 1754.
Dau. Ann Kendall at 18; Frances dau. of Samuel Kendall; Sarah dau. of Robert Frank; Borrington son of Robert Frank; Stephen son of John Bailey; wife Elizabeth.

JONES, NATHANIEL, gent., 21 Jan. 1753; 26 Mch. 1754.
Wife Sarah Howson Jones; sons John, David, Nathaniel, Charles and Calvert Jones; daughters Mary Peck, Frances Jones and Sarah Franklin.

RALLINS, JAMES, 19 Jan. 1754; 26 Mch. 1754.
Wife Grace and Augustine Weedon exors.

WATTS, JOHN, 4 Nov. 1749; 27 Mch. 1754.
Son John land in Westmoreland and King George; son Richard land in Prince William; to Beheathland Blagg my housekeeper; daughters Frances and Elizabeth Watts when 21; if my children marry a Maryland man or woman they are to forfeit their part of my estate; sister Margaret Grant; friends Charles Ashton, James Bankhead, James Berryman and George Gray exors.

BARNET, JOHN, 24 Feb. 1752; 30 Apl. 1754.
Son Richard; grandson Henry Barnet; dau. Elizabeth Finch; son John Finch; dau. Mary Barnet; godson Joseph Cockrell; wife Elizabeth.

FLING, WILLIAM, 25 Jan. 1754; 30 Apl. 1754.
To James Wilkerson; dau. Margaret decd.; three daughters Elizabeth Fling, Ann Wilkerson and Mary Wilkerson; sons in law Thomas and Robert Wilkerson exors.

RUST, WILLIAM, 26 Mch. 1754; 30 Apl. 1754.
Brother Samuel Rust; mentions father Jeremiah Rust; brother Jeremiah Rust; brother in law Thadeus Jackson.

HABORN, GEORGE, 10 July 1753; 30 July 1754.
Son George; wife Elender; children George, Jane, Elender and Desire; son James, James Baley and Thomas McFarlane exors

MIDDLETON, ROBERT, 20 Aug. 1739; 31 July 1754.
Two sisters Mary and Alice Middleton; coz. Thomas Middleton; brother Benjamin Middleton exor.

ARNOLD, WEEDON, 18 Jan. 1754; 27 Aug. 1754.
Two children James and John; wife Ann; I resign my Sheriff's office to friend Lovell Harrison; exors. Colonel Andrew Monroe, Capt. Robert Vaulx and Mr. Lawrence Butler.

JETT, JOHN, 29 Mch. 1754; 26 Nov. 1754.
Son John land in King George; sons Peter and Francis; daughters Mary, Elizabeth and Ann Jett.

RALLINS, BENJAMIN, ———; 28 Jan. 1755.
Brother Samuel Rallins; sister Mary Whiting; dau. Ann when 18; exor. John Whiting.

SUTTON, MARY, 17 Mch. 1755; 26 Mch. 1755.
Son Jacob; son in law William Hazelrigg; grandchildren Mary Sutton, Elizabeth Thomas, Henrietta Sutton, Kezia Haselrigg; to daughter Mary Haselrigg and Christian and Frances Sutton; to Richard Sutton and Elijah Sutton.

NEALE, MARGARET, 11 Oct. 1753; 27 May 1755.
Son Shapleigh Neale; dau. Jemima Neale; son Richard; dau. Elizabeth Spence; exors. son Daniel Neale and John Spence, Jnr.

JONCEL, EDWARD, 21 Apl. 1755; 27 May 1755.
To son John all estate; to Lionel and Robert Massey and to Lionel's children had by my sister; exors. John Balser and Thomas Taylor.

McKENNE, WILLIAM, 13 Jan. 1755; 29 July 1755.
Wife Elizabeth and after her death to all my children.

PRICE, EVAN, 22 June 1754; 29 June 1755.
Daughter Sarah Hutcheson; wife Sarah; son John plantation on which William Hutcheson now lives; son Evan; daughters Mary and Grace Price.

RUST, WINIFRED, 8 Aug. 1754; 29 July 1755.
To Vincent Rust my part of the plantation of my father which was divided between us Sarah, Frances and Mary Rust; my brother George Rust; sister Sarah Clator.

EDWARDS, WILLIAM, 18 Jan. 1755; 27 May 1755.
My sons George, Anthony, Arnold and Joseph; to John Burrus Settle on a/c of my daughter Mary Burrus Settle; dau. Grace Edwards; wife Elizabeth; son William; dau. Martha Naillor.

QUESENBURY, NICHOLAS, 2 May 1755; 26 Aug. 1755.
My dau. Ann Welch; the child my wife goes with; my father and my wife exors.

JACKSON, JOSEPH, 16 May 1751; 26 Aug. 1755.
Daughter Lettice Newton; my father Richard Jackson; brother John Jackson; nieces Ann Jackson and Elenor Thompson; brother Richard Jackson; brother John Jackson and John Thompson.

SPENCE, JEMIMA, 6 May 1755; 30 Sept. 1755.
Daughter Elizabeth Sandford; son Patrick Spence; daughter Jemima Suggett; dau. Mary Spence; son Youell Spence; grandchildren Jemima Suggett and Jemima Sandford.

McFARLANE, THOMAS, 17 Sept. 1755; 25 Nov. 1755.
To Elizabeth Cox; to Frances Wright; wife Elizabeth; my four daus. Mary, Jane, Ann and Hannah McFarlane when 18; exors. friends John Bushrod and Francis Wright.

DEANE, CHARLES, 26 Feb. 1784; 30 Nov. 1784.
Wife Mary; sister Lucy Nowel; daughter Anne Deane.

BUTLER, WILLIAM, 7 Oct. 1784; 30 Nov. 1784.
Wife Celia; my father and mother Nathaniel and Ann Butler; brother John Butler; my four sisters Hannah, Betsy, Nelly and Sally.

McKENNEY, GERRARD, 25 Nov. 1784; 30 Nov. 1784.
Daughter Lettice Porter; son Gerrard; daughter Diana McKenney; dau. Katy McKenney; dau. Sarah McKenney; son Armstrong.

FURGESON, MARGARET, 25 Oct. 1784; 25 Jan. 1785.
To William and Isaac Stone sons of my decd. brother George Stone the estate I am entitled to by the death of my husband.

SANFORD, MARGARET, 16 Dec. 1784; 22 Feb. 1785.
Sons Reuben and William; daughter Barbara Sanford; granddaughter Peggy Sanford.

DEATTERLEY, MATTHEW, 21 Jan. 1782; 22 Feb. 1785.
Wife Elizabeth; son George; youngest son Thomas; sons James and John.

POPE, JOHN, 29 Nov. 1784; 29 Mch. 1785.
My wife; sons Elliott, William, Ransdell, John and Thomas; to Capt. Benjamin Strother.

BUTLER, SARAH, 4 Nov. 1784; 26 Apl. 1785.
Brother Lawrence Butler; niece Elcey Butler; niece Jane Butler; brother Christopher Butler's children; sisters Joice and Jane Butler.

ATTWELL, RICHARD, 6 Feb. 1782; 28 June 1785.
Son William; my youngest son; wife Mary; my children.

BANKHEAD, JAMES, 8 Jan. 1785; 28 June 1785.
My wife and children; brothers William and John Bankhead; brothers in law William and Thomas Miller.

THOMSON, WILLIAM, 29 Jan. 1785; 28 June 1785.
Wife Ann; children Richard, Betsy, Lovel and Maria; son William; mother in law Margaret Thomson; daughter Margaret land of her grandfather Hales.

GREEN, WILLIAM, 3 Sept. 1783; 26 July 1785.
Wife Sarah; sons Burkett and Reuben; daughters Letty and Molly; son John; daughters Sarah and Margaret.

BENNETT, 12 Mch. 1785; 30 Aug. 1785.
Wife Mary.

BOWCOCK, THOMAS, 6 Aug. 1784; 30 Aug. 1785.
Daughters Sally Bowcock, Susanna Dowling, Elizabeth Spellman and Caty Bowcock; son Henry.

JETT, THOMAS, 14 Feb. 1785; 25 Oct. 1785.
Son William Storke Jett; dau. Ann Bernard; dau. Mary Storke; grandson Thomas Bernard; to Henry son of Lawrence Washington decd.; nephew Birkett Jett; wife Sukey; grandson Thomas Storke.

ASBURY, ANNE, 10 Nov. 1755; 25 Nov. 1755.
Son Thomas; dau. in law Ann Asbury; dau. Elizabeth Muse; to Jeremiah Muse; dau. Mary Rochester; granddaughter Anne Wright; to Henry Asbury, Coleman Asbury, Ann Asbury, Walker Muse, Penelope Muse, Nicholas Rochester and William Rochester.

PRICE, WILLIAM, 13 Oct. 1755; 30 Mch. 1756.
My daughters Betty, Jane, Katy and Patty Price; wife Jane.

BOOK XIII.

MOTHERSHEAD, CHARLES, 12 Apl. 1756; 25 May 1756.
My sister ———; my cousins Elizabeth and Thomas James; sister Mary Wilkerson; cousin Charles Wilkerson; bro. in law Thomas James.

ROBERSON, THOMAS, ———; 29 June 1756.
My wife Anne and son Richard; grandson John son of Thomas Roberson; grandson Thomas Redman Roberson; three sons William, John and James.

AWBREY, CHANDLER, 9 Dec. 1755; 25 Sept. 1756.
Son James at 21; dau. ——— Awbrey; to ———; wife Elizabeth; sister Hannah McAulay; niece Mary McAulay; Mrs. Elizabeth Atwell; Sarah Atwell; my children ———.

PRICE, EVAN, 3 Nov. 1755; 28 Sept. 1756.
To Valinda Bolthrop; brother John Price; my mother Sarah Price and my two sisters Mary and Grace Price; uncle Henry Field.

ROE, BUNCH, 26 July 1756; 28 Sept. 1756.
Nephew William Roe; to Susanna Baker; estate to Thomas Whiting's children; brother Henry Roe, William Munroe and John Weedon exors; to Butler Baker.

CLAYTOR, THOMAS, 27 Dec. 1750; 28 Sept. 1756.
Eldest son John; sons Thomas and Alvin; dau. Elizabeth Claytor; dau. Anne; sons William and Samuel; grandson William son of John.

COURTNEY, MARY, 5 July 1756; 26 Oct. 1756.
Son Samuel; dau. Rosamund Garner; granddau. Mary Garner; my four sons James, Leonard, Samuel and ——— Courtney; sons Leonard and Jeremiah exors.

ELLIOTT, JOHN, 25 May 1756; 26 Oct. 1756.
Three sons William, Robert and Augustine; my wife; to Capt. John Rouzee.

MIDDLETON, BENJAMIN, 10 Oct. 1756; 30 Nov. 1756.
Wife Jemima; children Mary, Alice, Benjamin, Jane and Elizabeth; dau. Mary Brown; dau. Alice Harrison; exors. wife and Wm. Middleton.

BUTLER, THOMAS, 13 Aug. 1756; 30 Nov. 1756.
Son John at 21; dau. Elizabeth Butler; to William Jackson and Sarah Jackson; to Ann Butler, Jr.; Thomas Butler exor.

BUTLER, THOMAS, 29 May 1756; 26 Apl. 1757.
To son James land given me by my father; sons William and John and the child my wife Isabel goes with; George Munroe exor.

STEPTOE, JAMES, gent., 10 May 1755; 28 June 1757.
Sons James, George and Thomas; dau. Ann; wife Elizabeth; dau. Elizabeth.

NAUGHTY, JAMES, 12 Apl. 1755; —— July 1757.
My father James Naughty; brother John; sister Mary Garrard and her two eldest children; exors. William Garrard and John Naughty.

VAULX, ROBERT, 8 Aug. 1754; 26 Mch. 1755.
Friend John Elliott and his two sons; daughters Milly and Molly Vaulx; daughters Katy and Kenner; to wife and the child she goes with; daughters Betty and Sally; to Brereton Kenner; the children of my present wife; my daughters by a former wife; to William Bernard my law books; to Thomas Shadrack; son in law Lawrence Washington.

DUNKIN, GEORGE, 31 Dec. 1757; 28 Feb. 1758.
Sisters Elizabeth and Sarah Dunkin; exor. Samuel Jackson, Snr.

WHITING, THOMAS, 6 Dec. 1757; 28 Mch. 1758.
Daughters Molly, Sally, Nelly and Lizzie Whiting; Mary wife of Samuel Dishman; Elizabeth wife of Spence Monroe.

RANSDELL, WHARTON, 10 June 1755; 25 Apl. 1758.
Son Edward; dau. Sarah Elliott Pierce; sons Wharton and William; wife Sarah.

RICE, ZERUBABEL, 19 May 1758; 30 May 1758.
Eldest son Zerubabel; 2nd son Simon; youngest son John; dau. Mary Rice; wife Isabella and all my children.

CALLES, WILLIAM, 20 Jan. 1758; 30 May 1758.
Two sons Garland and William Overton Calles; wife Mary.

BROWN, ORIGINAL, 29 Jan. 1744; 29 Nov. 1757.
To wife Elizabeth all estate.

BENNETT, WILLIAM, 18 Sept. 1758; 30 Jan. 1759.
Mother Elizabeth Bennett; brothers Charles, Daniel and Thomas Bennett.

NEALE, DANIEL, 28 Apl. 1758; 24 Apl. 1759.
My four sons Christopher, Presley, Richard and John; son Spence Neale; son Daniel Neale; son Rodham Neale land in Richmond co.; dau. Penny Spence Neale; brother Ramsdell and sons Spence, Daniel and Rodham exors.

ALLERTON, WILLOUGHBY, 30 June 1759; 25 Sept. 1759.
Wife Ann; to David Connier's two daughters my sisters in law Jane and Alice; to Capt. Hancock Eustace; to Richard Lee, Esq.

PIPER, JOHN, 12 Aug. 17 ——; 25 Sept. 1759.
Daughter Rachel and her husband William Munroe; son Jonathan Piper and his wife Ann and their son John; son David; son Thomas Muse and my dau. Ann his wife; son William and my dau. Mary Piper; youngest son Benjamin Piper.

SANFORD, RICHARD, 25 July 1757; 30 Oct. 1759.
Wife Susannah; to son Richard land in Fairfax where he now lives; son Robert; granddaughter Susannah dau. of my son Edward; dau. Frances Harrison; dau. Elizabeth Cox; dau. Ann Muse; kinsman Aug. Sanford; grandson Franklin Perry in full of his mother Susannah Perry decd.; grandson Richard Muse the part of his mother Mary Muse decd.; grandson Thomas Muse 1/- in full of his mother Sarah Muse decd.; three sons Richard, Robert and Edward exors.

BROWN, WILLIAM, 11 Aug. 1759; 30 Oct. 1759.
Son William; son John; dau. Mary Hord; dau. Jane Price; dau. Elizabeth Craighill; dau. Margaret Williams; dau. Hannah Butler.

CHANDLER, JOSEPH, 17 Mch. 1758; 29 Jan. 1760.
Sons Thomas and William; daus. Elizabeth and Mary Chandler; wife Frances; dau. Ann.

CORBIN, GAWIN, 9 Oct. 17———; 29 Jan. 1760.
Daughter Martha Corbin; brother Richard Corbin's two youngest sons; sister Tucker; godson Thomas son of Richard Henry Lee; wife Hannah.

SPILLMAN, WILLIAM, ———; 29 Apl. 1760.
Youngest dau. Margaret; sons Thomas, William and John; dau. Lettice Dulin.

POPE, HUMPHREY, 9 Aug. 1759; 27 May 1760.
Children John, Humphrey, Benjamin, Mary and Nathaniel Pope; wife Sarah.

LANE, WILLIAM, 19 Aug. 1758; 26 Aug. 1760.
Son James my plantation; son William Carr Lane; son Joseph; son James; dau. Hannah Middleton; wife Martha.

WILKINSON, TYLER, 6 Apl. 1758; 28 Oct. 1760.
Sons Tyler, William, James, Thomas, Gerrard and Robert; to Elizabeth Ribeto; wife Elizabeth.

SANFORD, ROBERT, 23 Aug. 1760; 28 Oct. 1760.
Son James; dau. Winifred Sanford; son Robert; son John; dau. Ann Moxley; dau. Jemima South.

BUSHROD, JOHN, gent., 14 Feb. 1760; 30 Dec. 1760.
Wife Mildred; granddau. Mary Washington; dau. Hannah Washington; granddaughter Jenny Washington; dau. Elizabeth Bushrod; to Lydia Bushrod Pettit dau. of Mr. John Pettit; friends Honl. Richard Corbin and Major John Washington exors.

PARTRIDGE, JANE, 18 Sept. 1760; 31 Mch. 1761.
To son ———; to son Ashton Lamkin; dau. Elener Cox; granddau. Sarah Rust; grandson Daniel Lamkin; son Matthew Partridge land in Culpeper county.

BOOK XIV.

WALKER, JOHN, 25 Sept. 1760; 31 Mch. 1761.
Wife Ann; three children William, James and Elizabeth Walker.

COURTNEY, SAMUEL, 18 July 1759; 31 Mch. 1761.
Godsons Samuel Courtney and Thomas Garner; brothers James, Leonard and Jeremiah Courtney and sister Rosannah Garner.

TODD, ROBERT, 18 Jan. 1761; 9 Apl. 1761.
To Richard Cadeen all my estate.

CHANCELLOR, THOMAS, 19 Nov. 1760; 31 Mch. 1761.
Children John, Catherine, Rebecca, Thomas and Sarah; wife Katherine.

JOHNSON, SAMUEL, 22 Dec. 1760; 31 Mch. 1761.
Granddaughters Ann, Margaret and Mary Johnson; to Mary dau. of Thomas Binks decd.; grandson Samuel Johnson; wife Ann and William Smith, exors.

VIVION, THOMAS, 10 Sept. 1760; 28 Apl. 1761.
To son Charles land in King George; son Francis; to my dau. Jane that I had by my late wife before marriage; daughter Mary; dau. Frances Brooking; dau. Margaret Pratt; friends Thomas Jett, John Orr and my two sons exors.

LOWE, JOHN, 6 Mch. 1761; 28 Apl. 1761.
My wife and children; George Hull and Bradley Garner exors.

ASHTON, BURDETT, 7 Mch. 1760; 29 July 1760.
Estate to nephew Burdett son of Charles and Sarah Ashton; to brother Charles Ashton; nephews Lawrence and John Ashton.

REDMAN, WILLIAM, 27 Nov. 1760; 26 May 1761.
Daughter Winifred; sons John and William; dau. Lettice; wife Frances.

MULLINS, RACHEL, 2 Feb. 1761; 26 May 1761.
To John Barber; daughter Rachel Mullins.

SETTLE, WILLIAM, 1 Oct. 1760; 26 May 1761.
Wife Sarah and son Joel.

ROSE, CHARLES, clerk, 7 Mch. 1760; 30 June 1761.
Sons Robert, John and Alexander; daughters Catherine and Molly Rose; wife Catherine; my brother Alexander and my nephew John Rose exors.

WILLIAMS, THOMAS, 20 May 1761; 30 June 1761.
Son Elijah; son Daniel; my wife and three children.

RUST, FRANCES, 23 July 1759; 30 June 1761.
Son Robert Middleton; dau. Rachel Cox; son Benjamin Rust; daughters Frances Shearman and Molly Rust.

GARNER, ABRAHAM, 21 Feb. 1761; 30 June 1761.
Daughters Frances, Sarah, Martha, Lettice and Rachel Garner.

ARISS, SPENCER, 23 Nov. 1760; 28 July 1761.
Wife Sarah; dau. Elizabeth Ariss; brother John Ariss; nephew John Ariss Calles; sister Sorrell.

TIDWELL, ROBERT, 27 Sept. 1757; 28 July 1761.
Wife Hannah; son William Carr Tidwell; dau. Elizabeth; **granddaughter** Hannah Tidwell; son John; to Katherine Jenkins.

MARMADUKE, CHRISTOPHER, 20 Jan. 1761; 28 July 1761.
Son Christopher and his son Vincent; son Daniel; dau. Esther Robinson; granddaughters Hannah and Elizabeth Holland; dau. Jemima Sandy; son

John; to Margaret Sandford; granddaughter Elizabeth Marmaduke; all my children Christopher, Jean, John, Daniel, Esther, William and Jemima.

BAXTER, EDWARD, 16 June 1761; 28 July 1761.
George son of William Monroe decd. as exor.; to George Monroe's daughter Mary; my two brothers George and Thomas Baxter.

NEWMARCH, JONATHON, 13 Nov. 1761; 26 Jan. 1762.
Son Thomas; son Jonathan; grandson William Brown; to Dorothy Tingle; dau. Elizabeth Brown and son in law James Brown.

NAUGHTY, JAMES, 22 Aug. 1761; 26 Jan. 1762.
To my daughter Mary Garrard; granddaughter Ann Garrard; granddau. Elizabeth Garrard; to Martha Brown; to John Briges; to Mary Brown; son John Naughty; grandson James Garrard.

SELF, WILLIAM, 10 Mch. 1761; 26 Jan. 1762.
Son William; grandson Peter and his brother William Self; dau. Susannah; Benjamin Hall's children; daughters Becky and Lettice; Stephen Self to live on my plantation and care for the bringing up of my children; son Abraham.

LEE, GEORGE, gent., 13 Sept. 1761; 26 Jan. 1762.
Eldest son George Fairfax Lee; sons Lancelot and William Lee; dau. Elizabeth Lee; friend Col. Richard Henry Lee; my late wife; to son Lancelot a seal with the family coat of arms cut thereon given me by Col. Richard Lee; friends Col. George William Fairfax, Col. Richard Henry Lee, Col. Richard Lee, William Bryant Fairfax and Capt. John Turberville to be guardians.

RUST, PETER, 9 Nov. 1761; 26 Jan. 1762.
To Daniel Lamkin land in Loudoun county; my four sons Richard, James, John and Peter; son Samuel; wife Elizabeth; daughters Mary, Martha, Hannah and Elizabeth.

DUNBAR, WILLIAM, 11 Nov. 1761; 23 Feb. 1762.
My three children Molly, James and William.

WHITE, SARAH, 26 Nov. 1761; 24 Feb. 1762.
Son John; dau. Jenney Smith; dau. Susannah White; dau. Margaret Mothershead.

BAKER, JOHN, 27 Nov. 1761; 30 Mch. 1762.
Wife Elizabeth; sons William and John and dau. Ann Baker.

NASH, ELIZABETH, ———; 30 Mch. 1762.
Daughter Ann Nash; son John Nash; son Thomas Brown; son Nathaniel Nash; dau. Elizabeth Bragg; son William Nash; son Jeremiah Nash.

SMITH, STEPHEN, Snr., 22 Nov. 1761; 30 Mch. 1762.
Son Samuel to be bound to his uncle George Banister; my wife and children; brother Samuel Smith and friend James Bailey exors.

MOORE, ROBERT, 5 Dec. 1761; 30 Mch. 1762.
Wife Elizabeth; sons John and Robin; dau. Eleanor Moore.

DAVIS, JOHN, 17 Jan. 1754; 30 Mch. 1762.
Son William; wife Jane and all my children.

BRANHAM, MICHAEL, 3 Dec. 1761; 27 Apl. 1762.
Son Barnaby; wife Rosannah and my children Ignatius, Barnaby, Joseph, William, Elizabeth and Rosannah.

WASHINGTON, AUGUSTINE, 18 Sept. 1758; 25 May 1762.
To son William Augustine at 21; my decd. brother Lawrence Washington; my three daughters Betty, Nancy and Jane; wife to be extx. with Fielding Lewis, Richard Henry Lee, and my brothers George and John Washington. Codicil. 16 Feb. 1762. My wife being delivered of a son George; my wife in descent from her grandfather Col. Ashton; my brothers Samuel and Charles; the children of my sister Lewis and the children of my sister in law Mrs. Booth; to Mrs. William Booth of Cople Parish.

COX, PETER PRESLEY, 6 June 1762; 29 June 1762.
Godson Richard Wright; goddaughter Molly Cox; to Jane Mussett's daughters Sally and Nancy; my brother Fleet Cox; my brother William Cox.

BANISTER, GEORGE, 21 May 1762; 29 June 1762.
Sister Ann Smith and her son Robert; brother in law John Baley and sister Elizabeth Baley.

LAMKIN, PETER, 2 Nov. 1757; 29 June 1762.
My sons Mathew, Peter, George and James; wife Ann.

QUISENBERRY, WILLIAM, Snr., 27 May 1762; 27 July 1762.
My daughter Eleanor Bayn; grandsons Nicholas Quisenberry, John Mothershead and William Dodd; son William Quisenberry; extx. my two daughters Ann and Elizabeth.

WHEELER, WILLIAM, 18 Nov. 1761; 28 Sept. 1762.
Wife Elizabeth; dau. Sarah Horton; dau. Elizabeth Strother; sons Thomas, Richard and John.

MOXLEY, ALEXANDER, 5 Aug. 1762; 28 Sept. 1762.
Wife Frances; brother John Moxley's son Rodham; cousin Joseph Moxley.

DAVIS, ELIZABETH, 20 May 1759; 25 Sept. 1762.
Sister Frances Davis; to Mary Davis.

PRITCHETT, THOMAS, 24 May 1762; 30 Nov. 1762.
Estate to my children; brother James Pritchett exor.

BALTHROP, JOHN, 28 Aug. 1762; 30 Nov. 1762.
Sons William and John; daughters Sarah, Elizabeth, Margaret and Nancy Balthrop; wife Jemima; sons Sharp and James.

BERRYMAN, ELIZABETH, 14 June 1762; 22 Feb. 1763.
My decd. husband Benjamin Berryman; my sons Newton, John and Henry all decd. before coming of age; sons William, James and Maximilian surviving; children William, James and Catherine Nowles; dau. Rose Taliaferro; dau. Frances Foot; dau. Sarah Douglass; dau. Catherine Nowles.

TEBBS, DANIEL, 25 May 1760; 20 Feb. 1762.
Son William; wife Elizabeth; son Daniel; daughters Mary and Elizabeth Tebbs.

HORE, JAMES, 12 Apl. 1763; 31 May 1763.
Godson Beckwith Butler; cousin Sarah Hore; to Elias Hore; to William Berkeley; godson John Berkeley; to Mary Nelson, Snr.; to godson William Nelson; to Mary Nelson, Jr.; to James son of my coz. Elias Hore the plantation I live on; to John Triplett.

MIDDLETON, MARY, 6 Mch. 1755; 27 Sept. 1763.
To William and Thomas the sons of Thomas Middleton decd.; Mary Brown dau. of my brother Benjamin Middleton; Leazure widow of Thomas Middleton decd. extx.

JEFFRIES, GEORGE, 30 Aug. 1763; 25 Oct. 1763.
Children William, John, George, Maria, Elizabeth and Ann; exors. Jeremiah Jeffries and my wife Elizabeth.

WHITE, JAMES, 21 Oct. 1762; 25 Oct. 1763.
To Alice Kersey; son Benjamin White's three daughters Jane, Mildred and Amy White; son John White's two sons Samuel and John; son Daniel; dau. Jemima Balthrop; dau. Verlinda Grigsby; son James; granddaughter Winifred Balthrop.

WEEDON, AUGUSTINE, 21 Sept. 1763; 29 Nov. 1763.
My daughters Elizabeth, Jane and Rebecca Weedon; dau. Mary Hilton; sons John, George and Augustine; dau. Sarah.

DAVIS, FRANCES, 16 Nov. 1763; 29 Nov. 1763.
Sisters Anne, Mary and Katherine Davis.

DAVIS, ANNE, 12 Oct. 1763; 29 Nov. 1763.
Daughter Anne Davis; my five daughters; daus. Anne and Mary extx.

WILKERSON, JOHN, 21 Feb. 1764; 27 Mch. 1764.
Sons Benjamin and John; wife Margaret.

BAKER, JOHN, 10 Feb. 1764; 27 June 1764.
Daughters Frances and Winney; wife Katherine; sons James, Samuel, Richard; dau. Rebecca.

TIDWELL, HANNAH, 27 Jan. 1760; 29 May 1764.
Hannah dau. of son John Tidwell; grandchildren Elizabeth and Barbara Tidwell; dau. Elizabeth Tidwell; son William Carr Tidwell exor.

LEE, MARY, of Lee Hall, 19 Oct. 1762; 29 May 1764.
Daughter Lettice Ball; son Richard; granddaughter Mary Ball; sons John, Richard and Henry Lee; daughters in law Mary and Lucy Lee; grandsons William and Henry Lee Ball; son Richard Lee exor.

BAKER, BUTLER, 21 Jan. 1764; 26 June 1764.
Sons William and Samuel; daus. Elizabeth, Frances and Susannah.

HARRISON, SAMUEL, 11 Aug. 1763; 31 July 1764.
Son William; my father George Harrison decd.; son Jeremiah; daus. Ann and Hannah Harrison; wife Magdalene.

DAVIS, ANNE, 9 Jan. 1764; 28 Aug. 1764.
Sister Esther Davis; sisters Katherine and Mary Davis.

OMOHUNDRO, JOHN, 16 Jan. 1765; 26 Feb. 1765.
Sons Thomas, William, John and Richard; son in law Joseph Taylor; dau. Jemima Weaver; dau. Elizabeth Davis and Grandson Jesse Davis.

WHITE, MARY, 20 Oct. 1764; 26 Feb. 1765.
Granddaughter Anne Porter; dau. Sarah Russell; granddaughter Mary dau. of Philip White; son George White; Griffin Garland exor; dau. Anne Walker; Granddaughter Elizabeth Reynolds.

FINCH, JOHN, 2 Jan. 1765; 26 Feb. 1765.
Brother Nicholas Muse; sister Mary Randall; sister Anne Muse; brother in law Thomas Randall.

HILTON, JOHN, 24 Sept. 1764; 28 May 1765.
Son William; dau. Mary; dau. Elizabeth at 21.

MASSEY, LOVELL, 3 June 1764; 28 May 1765.
Wife Martha; sons Lovell and James; dau. Judith Massey; dau. Mildred; dau. Frances Spilman; son Robert.

GILBERT, MICHAEL, 13 Feb. 1765; 25 June 1765.
Son William; dau. Sarah Morton; son Thomas; wife Mary and all my children.

DELOZIER, THOMAS, 24 Dec. 1764; 30 July 1765.
Wife Susannah; son Richard Davis Delozier; dau. Molly Randall Delozier; son Daniel.

KIRK, JOHN, 11 Dec. 1764; 27 Aug. 1765.
Wife Sarah; son John and the rest of my children.

CHILTON, THOMAS, 4 Sept. 1765; 24 Sept. 1765.
Son Thomas; dau. Mary Ransdall; grandson Chilton Ransdell; dau. Hannah Sturman; granddaughter Jemima Sturman; my three sons William, John and Charles land in Fauquier; son Stephen land in Prince William.

WASHINGTON, ROBERT, 11 Feb. 1763; 24 Sept. 1765.
Daughter Sukey and son John Washington; grandchildren Robert Townshend Washington and Sarah Washington; William Bernard to be guardian to dau. Sukey.

PIPER, JONATHAN, 18 Sept. 1763; 29 July 1766.
Son John; dau. Nancy Piper; children Susannah, Jenny, Rachel; wife Anne.

HODGSON, WILLIAM, 31 July 1765; 29 July 1766.
To Katherine Baker all my estate.

GOFF, WILLIAM O'BRIEN, 19 July 1766; 30 Sept. 1766.
Daughter Frances Johnstone land in Prince William; sons Benjamin and William; wife Jane.

BENNETT, COSSOM, 14 July 1765; 30 Sept. 1766.
Sons William and Bunbury; wife Catherine and my children.

HURLEY, JOHN, 31 Jan. 1766; 30 Sept. 1766.
Son John and wife Beheathland.

COX, PRESLEY, 18 Feb. 1766; 30 Sept. 1766.
Son Fleet Cox; grandsons Richard and Presley Wright; granddau. Nancy Wright; grandchildren Fleet, Presley and Molly Cox; son William; exor. Francis Wright.

JEFFRIES, JEREMIAH, 1 May 1766; 28 Oct. 1766.
Brother Robert Jeffries; to William Coward his freedom; wife Sarah.

SANFORD, WINIFRED, 27 Sept. 1766; 28 Oct. 1766.
Son William; to Ann South; Elizabeth wife of Peter Walker; sister Ann Moxley; exors. John South and Joseph Moxley.

LEE, JOHN, gent., of county of Essex; 23 Sept. 1765; 24 Feb. 1767.
Wife Mary; cousin Hancock Lee son of John Lee, Jnr., land in Essex; my brother Henry Lee land in Westmoreland; to nephew Henry Lee; brother Richard Lee; sister Lettice Ball; niece and nephew Mary and Henry Lee Ball; to Mary and Fanny daughters of Baldwin Mathews Smith; to Lettice, Philip, Mary and Elizabeth the children of John Lee, Jr.

NEWTON, JOHN, 8 Jan. 1767; 24 Feb. 1767.
Son Willoughby; the child my wife goes with.

VIGAR, WILLIAM, ———; 31 Mch. 1767.
Wife Sarah Vigar; daughter Frances; my six sons.

FLEMING, WILLIAM, 7 Jan. 1767; 28 Apl. 1767.
Wife Abigail; sons John and William; daughter Elizabeth wife of Thaddeus Jackson; daughter Peggy wife of Rodham Pritchett; dau. Martha Fleming.

SEARS, EDWARD, 4 July 1766; 28 Apl. 1767.
Wife Mary; son William; my children.

NEWTON, WILLOUGHBY, 7 Dec. 1766; 26 May 1767.
Son John land in Westmoreland; grandson Richard Jackson; dau. Judith Brent when she marries Brererton Kennar; William Jett and Katherine his wife; daughter Katherine Lane; son in law Thomas Lawson and his wife Lettice; son in law John Berryman and Martha his wife; son in law Benjamin Berryman and Sarah his wife; dau. Elizabeth Newton; dau. Mary Newton;

granddaughters Elizabeth Ashton and Ann Jackson. Codicil 6 Jan. 1767. To grandson Willoughby son of John Newton; to Betty widow of my son John who has died before me.

WEEDON, JANE, 15 Dec. 1763; 28 July 1767.
Estate to sisters Elizabeth, Rebecca and Sarah Weedon.

SPARK, WILLIAM, Par. of St. Thomas, Co. of Surry and Isle of Jamaica; 1 Jan. 1764; 25 Aug. 1767.
My mother Margaret Duthrie of Arbuthinck, Kincardine, Scotland; my three sisters Jane, Rebecca and Mary of same place; to brother Alexander Spark, merchant in Westmoreland Co., Va., all estate in Jamaica, etc.

JACKSON, MAGDALENE, 11 Aug. 1766; 24 Nov. 1767.
My beloved son Samuel; son Julius; son Thaddeus; son Christopher; my decd. husband Christopher D. Jackson.

HUTCHESON, WILLIAM, 14 Apl. 1767; 29 Mch. 1768.
Daughter Mary Hutcheson; wife Elizabeth.

PORTER, WILLIAM, 27 Dec. 1767; 28 Mch. 1768.
Sons Edward and William; daughters Ann, Sarah and Betty Porter.

CRUTCHER, JOHN, 4 Sept. 1767; 26 Apl. 1768.
Wife Susanna; sons John, Thomas and Joseph; dau. Susanna.

WHITE, JAMES, 3 Jan. 1768; 31 May 1768.
To Elizabeth Weedon; son George.

ROWE, WILLIAM, 12 May 1768; 27 Sept. 1768.
Daughter Jane Pope Rowe; granddaughter Elizabeth Fox; daughter Angelica Fox; son in law Joseph Fox; my wife.

BEARD, GEORGE, 12 Sept. 1768; 27 Sept. 1768.
Wife Nanna; daughter Susanna and son George Beard; my mother Ann Hilton; exors. William Smith and William Hilton.

BOOK XV.

BUTLER, ANN, 13 Sept. 1763; 27 Nov. 1768.
Daughter Elizabeth Sanford and after her death to her son William and her dau. Frances Sanford; granddaughter Sarah dau. of Mary Sanford; granddaughter Ann Sanford; grandsons John and William Butler; granddaughter Ann Henry; grandson William son of James Butler; friend Hannah Harrison dau. of Lovell Harrison; son in law Willoughby Sanford.

READE, RUTH, 4 Oct. 1768; 29 Nov. 1768.
Daughter Mary Reade; grandson Andrew Reade.

NAUGHTY, JOHN, 24 Nov. 1768; 29 Nov. 1768.
To Martha and Mary Brown; to John Bridges son of above Martha Brown and to his dau. Patty Bridges; to James Thomas; to Anne dau. of William Garrard; to godson Yelverton Quisenberry; to John son of William Berkeley; godson William Payne; godson John son of William Bridges; godson Richard Garrard son of Nathaniel Garrard.

MIDDLETON, JEREMIAH, 26 Dec. 1768; 30 May 1769.
Son George land in Richmond and Northumberland cos; son John; my wife Sarah Ellen and my four children.

GRACE, WILLIAM, 6 Sept. 1769; 28 Nov. 1769.
Wife Ann; son Thomas; dau. Ann Bell; son John; son William; son James.

CALLES, FRANCIS, 6 Sept. 1769; 27 Feb. 1770.
Brother Robert; wife Jane; my children; exors. Richard, Ambrose and Thomas Calles.

MIDDLETON, SARAH ELLEN, 23 July 1769; 27 Feb. 1770.
My decd. husband's directions to be observed in the disposition of my will.

GARNER, BRADLEY, 13 Oct. 1769; 26 June 1770.
To son George the land my father left me and the land bought of Samuel Garner after his mother's decease; son Vincent the land in North Carolina; daughter Elenor Garner; wife Catherine; my daughters Lettice Garner, Hannah Cox, Elizabeth Garner; sons Benjamin and Jeremiah; to Frances Garner dau. of Abraham Garner.

ATTWELL, JOHN, Apl. 1770; 26 June 1770.
Sons Thomas, John, Richard and Francis; daughters Elizabeth Lafon, Sarah Coghill and Martha Attwell; brother Francis Attwell; son Youell Attwell; son William; my wife.

JACKSON, DANIEL, 2 May 1767; 31 July 1770.
My five children, George, Daniel, William, Elizabeth Franklin and Sarah Jackson.

THOMPSON, ANDREW, 5 Sept. 1769; 28 Aug. 1770.
Daughter Mary; sons George and Andrew; daughters Margaret, Sarah, Beheathland and Winifred.

HUTT, GERRARD, 4 May 1770; 25 Sept. 1770.
Wife Mary; grandson William Hutt; grandson Gerrard Hutt; grandson Joseph son of Andrew Read; daughter Mary Ann Read; son Gerrard Hutt and his son Gerrard; grandson John son of William Brown.

SANFORD, THOMAS, 24 May 1767; 27 Nov. 1770.
Grandson Thomas son of Youell and Elizabeth Sanford; wife Margaret; grandson Thomas Luttrell; son Thomas.

MUSE, JOHN, 11 Oct. 1770; 27 Nov. 1770.
Exors. Richard and Daniel Muse; my two sons Daniel and James; wife Elenor.

MONROE, ANDREW, 1 May 1769; 27 Nov. 1770.
My wife Margaret; to grandson Elliott Monroe land in Loudoun; grandson John Monroe land where my son John lived; four grandchildren John, Jane, Elizabeth and Nancy Monroe; exors. Dr. James Bankhead, John Ashton and Spence Monroe.

PARTRIDGE, MATHEW, 13 Nov. 1770; 26 Mch. 1771.
Sons Richard and Mathew; daughters Sally, Jenny and Patty; wife Jemima; exor. Daniel Morgan.

HIGDON, JOHN, 23 Dec. 1770; 26 Mch. 1771.
Son John; children Elizabeth, Original, John and Richard Higdon.

LAWRENCE, CHARLES, 1 May 1770; Mch. 1771.
Cousin William Lawrence, Jr., all my estate.

MIDDLETON, BENEDICT, son of Robert Middleton; 22 Sept. 1770; 26 Mch. 1771.
My brothers John, William and Robert; my two cousins Mary and Elizabeth Rust.

BROWN, ELIZABETH, 30 Aug. 1770; 28 May 1771.
Brother James Dishman; sister Mary Rutherford.

CUPINGHEIFFER, JOHN, 13 Feb. 1770; 28 May 1771.
Wife Mary; children Mical, Hannah and John; brother Jacob exor.

BAYNE, MATHEW, Snr., 2 Mch. 1769; 17 Oct. 1771.
My wife Elenor; son Mathew; son Carson; daughter Sarah Vigor and her husband William; son William; son Richard and his dau. Mary Bayne; sons John, Daniel and George; dau. Any Bridges and her son Mathew; dau. Elizabeth Bayne.

MONROE, GEORGE, Jnr., 12 Nov. 1770; 25 June 1771.
Wife Peggy; sons George, John and William; daughters Mary, Sarah and Ann; brother William Monroe and friend Spence Monroe exors.

WEAVER, ADAM, 30 Nov. 1770; 25 June 1771.
Wife Annaminos; children John, William, Abraham, Benjamin, Vicarius, Elizabeth Bott, Mary Mothershead and Hannah Weaver; sons in law William Walker and William Iglis.

MIDDLETON, ROBERT, 22 Feb. 1771; 24 Sept. 1771.
My wife Elizabeth; when my youngest child is 16 years old.

McCLANAHAN, WILLIAM, 15 Sept. 1760; 29 Oct. 1771.
Wife Martha; to son in law Garland Moore land in Richmond co.; grandchildren Robert, Garland, Peter, McClanahan and Martha Moore; my five sons Thomas, Peter, William, James and John McClanahan.

STONE, JOSEPH, 16 Dec. 1770; 26 Nov. 1771.
Son Thomas, wife Ann, son Presley and the child my wife goes with; daughter Jemima Neale; dau. Penelope Stone; exors. wife Ann, Thomas Stone and Rodham Neale.

MOXLEY, JOHN, 14 Aug. 1771; 26 Nov. 1771.
My wife Elizabeth; son Augustine.

STOWERS, SAMUEL, 24 Dec. 1762; 31 Oct. 1771.
Cousin Samuel Stowers; wife Ann.

BULGER, JOHN, 23 Dec. 1771; 31 Dec. 1771.
Daughter Barbara Jenkins; dau. Elizabeth Parsons; children Johnson, Sally and Nancy Bulger.

BROWN, JOHN, 14 May 1770; 31 Dec. 1771.
To son William the land that came to me by William Fryer decd.; son John; dau. Priscilla Brown; my seven daughters.

CAVENDER, HENRY, 24 Dec. 1771; 31 Mch. 1772.
Daughter Ann Davis; wife Elizabeth; sons Thomas and John; dau. Rachael Nash.

READ, MARY, 21 Jan. 1772; 31 Mch. 1772.
Sister Ann Asbury; niece Barbara Hutt; nephew Andrew Read and his son Joseph; brother Richard Read.

MONROE, THOMAS, 9 Mch. 1772; 28 Apl. 1772.
Brothers Andrew and James Monroe; sisters Martha and Jane.

MIDDLETON, ALICE, 27 Oct. 1766; 28 Apl. 1772.
To Thomas son of Thomas Middleton decd.; William son of Thomas Middleton decd.; exors. James Walker and William Middleton.

SMITH, JOHN, 7 Jan. 1771; 28 Apl. 1772.
Sons John, Edward and Matthew Smith.

HOLLAND, YOUELL, 7 Dec. 1771; 25 May 1772.
Wife Hannah; dau. Rockey Holland.

HALL, LEASURE, 7 Jan. 1770; ——— 1772.
My dau. Ann Lewis; dau. Mary Bailey; brother Ashton Hall; wife Joanna Lewis Hall.

BERKELEY, WILLIAM, aged 45; 2 Nov. 1769; 28 July 1772.
Wife Peggy; son John at 21.

COLLINGSWORTH, JOHN, 9 Oct. 1766; 28 July 1772.
Nephews John and Thomas Collingsworth; sons Thomas, John, Jesse and Vincent; daughters Sarah, Peggy and Martha Collingsworth; wife Margaret.

HARRISON, JOHN, 4 Apl. 1769; 25 Aug. 1772.
The heirs of my son George Harrison; son John; dau. Abigail Harrison; son Robert; grandson Robert Harper.

MUSE, JOHN, 5 Jan. 1772; 29 Dec. 1772.
Sons Nicholas, James, Thomas and John; dau. Mary Muse.

HUTT, JOHN, 3 Dec. 1772; 29 Dec. 1772.
Sons John, William and Gerrard Robinson Hutt; to Gerrard Robinson; dau. Elizabeth R. Hutt; brother Gerrard Hutt.

NASH, JOHN, 24 Feb. 1773; 30 Mch. 1773.
To Solomon Billings; my wife Ann.

LAMKIN, GEORGE, 22 Dec. 1772; 30 Mch. 1773.
Wife Agnes; dau. Lucy; son Youell.

CARPENTER, WILLIAM, 23 Mch. 1773; 31 Mch. 1773.
To sister Ann Carpenter.

TAYLOR, THOMAS, 25 Sept. 1768; 25 May 1773.
To Jane wife of Thomas Burne; to Judith, Letty and John Stephens.

BERRYMAN, JAMES, 25 Jan. 1772; 27 July 1773.
To son James land in Maryland; daughters Caty, Frances and Sarah; sons James, John, Samuel and Newton; wife Sarah.

BOOK XVI.

MOXLEY, DANIEL, 18 May 1774. No date of probate.
Wife Mary; friend Capt. Thomas Chilton; Mr. William Chilton; nephew Richard Moxley, Jr., son of my brother Richard; nephew Joseph son of my brother Joseph; to Daniel son of my nephew Joseph the latter being son of my brother Joseph; to Daniel son of my nephew Richard Moxley, Jr.; to Richard son of my nephew Richard; to nephew William son of my brother John; to William son of my brother John.

McCLANAHAN, PETER, 9 Jan. 1775. No date of probate.
To son William and the rest of my six children, Peter, Thomas, James, Mary, Betty and John.

PINCKARD, THOMAS, 4 Dec. 1776. No date of probate.
My wife and sons George Weedon alias Pinckard and Thomas Pinckard.

COLLINS, JOHN, Snr., 30 June 1773; ——— Mch. 1776.
Daughter Elizabeth Rigg; daughter Jemima Brion; sons Charles and John.

SMITH, SPENCE, 18 Aug. 1775. No date of probate.
Son Samuel; wife Elizabeth; son Fleet Smith; daughter Katy Neale; daughters Jane and Polly Smith.

BAILEY, JOHN, Snr., 11 Jan. 1776; 26 Mch. 1776.
Son Stephen; wife Elizabeth; daughter Ann and her husband Markham Marshall; sons John and James Bailey; grandson Stephen Bailey.

FRANK, ROBERT, 8 Feb. 1776; 24 Sept. 1776.
Son James; grandson James Frank; wife Mary; son Robert.

DEGGES, JAMES, 28 Dec. 1777; 27 Feb. 1778.
Nephew Christopher Edrington; nieces Ann, Elizabeth and Susanna Edrington; nephew James Degges Dishman; my sister Harrison's daughter Elizabeth.

JORDAN, ROBERT, 22 Jan. 1776; 24 Sept. 1776.
Son Reuben; daughter Ann Rochester and her husband John Rochester.

DOZER, THOMAS, 23 Feb. 1770; 29 June 1779.
Wife Sarah; sons Thomas and Joseph; brother Richard Dozer.

JORDAN, REUBEN, 7 Dec. 1776; 26 Aug. 1777.
To godson Longworth son of Burges Longworth; godson William Rice; nephew William Rochester; niece Betsy Rochester; brother in law John Rochester; sister Ann Rochester; nephews Robert and John Rochester; wife Ann Jordan.

71

EDWARDS, THOMAS, 11 June 1774; 29 Nov. 1774.
Sons William and Thomas; daughter Mary S. Edwards; daughters Frankey and Alice Edwards; wife Alice.

SMITH, PETER, Snr., 9 Aug. 1774. No date of probate.
My daughters Mary, Nancy, Sallie and Susan; to Sarah widow of my brother James Smith; Hannah wife of Benedict Middleton, Snr.; brother William Smith.

COX, PRESLEY, 18 Feb. 1766; 30 Sept. 1766.
Son Fleet Cox; grandsons Richard and Presley Wright and granddaughter Nancy Wright; grandchildren Fleet, Presley and Molly Cox; son William.

DAVENPORT, JAMES, 30 April 1775; 26 Aug. 1777.
All estate to my wife.

CRABB, JOHN, 23 Jan. 1775; 27 April 1779.
Daughter Elizabeth Rogers Middleton; son John; daughter Mary Bennett; son Benedict; daughter Jane Middleton; daughter Lettice Crabb; son William.

FEAGIN, WILLIAM, 23 July. No date of probate.
Wife Ann; children James, George, Thomas and Betty Feagin.

NASH, JEREMIAH, 10 Nov. 1773. No date of probate.
Son Solomon; daughter Mary Ann McKenny; daughter Lydia Nash; daughter Anne Jones.

WASHINGTON, LAWRENCE, 4 Dec. 1773; 29 Mch. 1774.
Wife Susannah; daughters Elizabeth Storke and Katy Washington; son Henry; brother in law William Storke Jett; my sisters Elizabeth, Ann and Mary Jett; friend John Ashton Snr.

GARNER, JOSEPH, 25 Aug. 1775; 24 Sept. 1776.
Sons Joseph, Benjamin and Nathaniel; daughters Catherine Courtney; Mary Jeffries and Keziah Courtney; grandson Gawin Garner; granddaughter Elizabeth Barecroft; son Joseph Garner and William Barecroft exors.

BLUNDELL, ABSALOM, 1 April 1774. No date of probate.
Sons John and William; daughters Sarah and Sukey Blundell; wife Susanna; son Thomas; daughter Ann Blundell; son Absolom; to Molly Randall Delozier.

PORTER, ELENDER, 16 Jan. 1778; 31 Aug. 1779.
Son William Davis; daughter Sarah Headley; daughter Rachel Porter.

ROBINSON, HANNAH, 28 July 1778; 29 Sept. 1778.
Sister Apphia Dangerfield; nephew John Pettit; exors. Beckwith Butler and John Pettit.

BLUNDELL, SUSANNAH, 18 Nov. 1776; 25 Mch. 1777.
Daughter Molly Randall Delozier; daughter Sukey Blundell; son Daniel Delozier; children Richard Davis Delozier, Daniel Delozier, Molly Randall Delozier and Sukey Blundell.

QUSENBERRY, ANN, 23 Aug. 1773; 29 June 1779.
Sister Elizabeth Qusenberry; cousin William Dodd.

FLOOD, WILLIAM, 9 April 1775; 27 June 1775.
Son William at 21; son Nicholas; my brother Nicholas; grandson Walter
Jones; to son William my seal with my coat of arms on it; daughter Alice
Jones; daughter Elizabeth; godson Richard Parker, Jnr.

TEBBS, DANIEL, 25 Feb. 1776; 26 Mch. 1776.
Children Martha, William, Elizabeth, Foushee and Daniel Tebbs; wife Elizabeth; brother William Tebbs.

BUTLER, WILLIAM, 5 Sept. 1774. No date of probate.
Brother John Butler; sister Jesse (?) Butler; my nephews Thomas and John
sons of Benjamin Steward.

BROWN, WILLIAM, 26 Sept. 1774; 24 Sept. 1776.
To son John land in Loudoun co.; daughter Mary Williams; daughters Jane,
Hannah, Elizabeth and Sally Brown; son William.

SMITH, SAMUEL, 3 July 1776; 31 Dec. 1776.
My wife; brothers William and Stephen Smith; son William; dau. Melia
Modiset; grandson Samuel Parsley; daughter Jane Parsley; to James
Parsley; daughter Alice Smith; sons John, George Bailey and Stephen Smith.

MASSEY, JAMES, 27 Dec. 1777; 25 Aug. 1778.
Wife Sarah all estate.

SMITH, JOHN, 22 Nov. 1777; 24 Nov. 1778.
Wife Elizabeth; sons John, Augustine and Lewis; my small children; my
daughters.

RANSDELL, SARAH, 8 Oct. 1778; 27 Mch. 1781.
Daughter Sarah Elliott Pierce; granddaughter Martha Pierce; grandson
Elliott Sturman; son in law Joseph Pierce.

WALKER, JAMES, 31 Dec. 1777; 30 June 1778.
Son James now in Gt. Britain when he is 21; my two brothers Thomas and
John Walker; friend William Pierce; friend John Warden.

QUISENBERRY, HUMPHREY, 30 Jan. 1773; 24 Sept. 1776.
My wife Elizabeth and the three children by my present wife, viz: Elizabeth,
Peggy and John Quisenberry; daughter Ann Piper; dau. Mary Marshall;
daughter Elizabeth Burshaw; son in law John Pope.

BOWCOCK, ANTHONY, 15 Nov. 1777; 25 Nov. 1777.
Cousin John Bowcock; cousins Richard and Henry Bowcock; brother
Thomas Bowcock; cousin Mary Ann Bowcock daughter of James Bowcock,
decd.

MOORE, JANE, 5 Sept. 1775. No date of probate.
Son James Moore; daughter Dorcas Moore; to Hannah Moore; to Jane
Lamkin Moore; to Samuel Lamkin Moore; son Garland Moore.

MOXLEY, RICHARD, 5 Jan. 1776; 27 May 1777.
Son Richard; daughter Mary Leftwich; grandchildren Daniel Moxley, Catey Moxley, Mary Moxley and Nancy Leftwich; son Alvin Moxley.

BAYN, WILLIAM, 15 Feb. 1778; 27 Oct. 1778.
Son John; wife Elizabeth.

BUTLER, LAWRENCE, 18 Nov. 1773; 29 July 1777.
Children Joice, Sarah, Elizabeth, Jane, Christopher, John, Griffin and Lawrence Butler; wife Eleanor.

CARTER, ROBERT, 20 May 1776; 29 June 1779.
Grandfather Benjamin Tasker late of Maryland decd.; grandmother Ann Tasker decd.; to my father Robert Carter, Esq., all my estate.

HARRISON, DANIEL, 12 July 1774; 26 Mch. 1782.
Son William Lewis; son Willoughby; wife Eleanor; my five children William Lewis, Sally, Willoughby, Daniel and James Harrison; brother Joshua Harrison.

GILBERT, JANE, 11 Jan. 1778; 31 Mch. 1778.
Daughter Agnes Harrison; son Youel Rust; granddaughter Nancy.

HILTON, WILLIAM, 17 Dec. 1777; 27 Jan. 1778.
Son John; wife Mary and all my children.

HAILEY, RICHARD, 20 Sept. 1774. No date of probate.
To son John and Anthony Garrard; to John son of Frances Tupman; my decd. wife; to grandson the eldest son of Mary Rush; grandson Richard Garrard when he is 21, who is the eldest son of Anthony Garrard by my daughter.

HUNTER, JAMES, 6 Oct. 1777; 30 June 1778.
To wife Winifred if she remain unmarried until 1788 when my son John will be 21 the 3rd of Sept. of that year; sons William and James; all my children.

SMITH, SARAH, 21 Jan. 1779; 30 Mch. 1779.
Nephew and niece Gregory and Lucy Smith; brother Edward Smith; niece Mary Jacqueline Smith daughter of my sister Mary Smith; niece Ann Smith dau. of the same; niece Sarah Smith dau. of the same; sister Martha Jacqueline Smith; brothers John and Edward Smith and the Rev. Thomas Smith exors.

WROE, ORIGINAL, 21 Apl. 1772; 31 May 1774.
Sons William, Richard, Benjamin, John, Thomas and Reginald; daughter Judith Briggs until David Briggs shall come of age; daughter Elizabeth Scott; daughter Susanna Edwards; daughter Lucetta Wroe.

MONROE, SPENCE, 16 Feb. 1774. No date of probate.
To sons James and Spence; son in law William Buckner; sons Andrew and Joseph Jones; exors. brother in law Joseph Jones and James Bankhead, Snr.; daughter Elizabeth Buckner.

BUTLER, THOMAS, 29 May 1756; 26 Apl. 1757.
To son James land given me by my father; sons William and John and the child my wife Isabel goes with; George Munroe exor.

STEPTOE, JAMES, gent., 10 May 1755; 28 June 1757.
Sons James, George and Thomas; dau. Ann; wife Elizabeth; dau. Elizabeth.

NAUGHTY, JAMES, 12 Apl. 1755; ——— July 1757.
My father James Naughty; brother John; sister Mary Garrard and her two eldest children; exors. William Garrard and John Naughty.

VAULX, ROBERT, 8 Aug. 1754; 26 Mch. 1755.
Friend John Elliott and his two sons; daughters Milly and Molly Vaulx; daughters Katy and Kenner; to wife and the child she goes with; daughters Betty and Sally; to Brereton Kenner; the children of my present wife; my daughters by a former wife; to William Bernard my law books; to Thomas Shadrack; son in law Lawrence Washington.

DUNKIN, GEORGE, 31 Dec. 1757; 28 Feb. 1758.
Sisters Elizabeth and Sarah Dunkin; exor. Samuel Jackson, Snr.

WHITING, THOMAS, 6 Dec. 1757; 28 Mch. 1758.
Daughters Molly, Sally, Nelly and Lizzie Whiting; Mary wife of Samuel Dishman; Elizabeth wife of Spence Monroe.

RANSDELL, WHARTON, 10 June 1755; 25 Apl. 1758.
Son Edward; dau. Sarah Elliott Pierce; sons Wharton and William; wife Sarah.

RICE, ZERUBABEL, 19 May 1758; 30 May 1758.
Eldest son Zerubabel; 2nd son Simon; youngest son John; dau. Mary Rice; wife Isabella and all my children.

CALLES, WILLIAM, 20 Jan. 1758; 30 May 1758.
Two sons Garland and William Overton Calles; wife Mary.

BROWN, ORIGINAL, 29 Jan. 1744; 29 Nov. 1757.
To wife Elizabeth all estate.

BENNETT, WILLIAM, 18 Sept. 1758; 30 Jan. 1759.
Mother Elizabeth Bennett; brothers Charles, Daniel and Thomas Bennett.

NEALE, DANIEL, 28 Apl. 1758; 24 Apl. 1759.
My four sons Christopher, Presley, Richard and John; son Spence Neale; son Daniel Neale; son Rodham Neale land in Richmond co.; dau. Penny Spence Neale; brother Ramsdell and sons Spence, Daniel and Rodham exors.

ALLERTON, WILLOUGHBY, 30 June 1759; 25 Sept. 1759.
Wife Ann; to David Connier's two daughters my sisters in law Jane and Alice; to Capt. Hancock Eustace; to Richard Lee, Esq.

PIPER, JOHN, 12 Aug. 17 ———; 25 Sept. 1759.
Daughter Rachel and her husband William Munroe; son Jonathan Piper and his wife Ann and their son John; son David; son Thomas Muse and my dau. Ann his wife; son William and my dau. Mary Piper; youngest son Benjamin Piper.

JETT, ANN, 10 Sept. 1781; 25 Sept. 1781.
Grandson Birkett; granddaughter Anne Bernard; grandson William Storke
Jett; son Thomas.

HEABRON, JAMES, 16 Mch. 1781; 25 Sept. 1781.
Son George; daughter Frances Lambert; son William; wife Elizabeth and
children Jane Conelly, Nancy Heabron, Betsy Heabron and James Heabron.

TAYLOR, MARY, 7 Oct. 1781; 27 Nov. 1781.
Son Thomas Scutt; son Charles Scutt; daughter Mary Morse.

WROE, WILLIAM, 18 Jan. 1781; 27 Nov. 1781.
Son Original land in King George; son William land in Culpeper; my six
children William, Katherine, Elenor, Rebecca, Jenny and Gracey; wife Grace.

PIERCE, WILLIAM, 7 Feb. 1782; 26 Feb. 1782.
Son Joseph; daughter Ellen Lawson; daughter Molly Gordon; wife Sarah.

WIGLEY, JOB, 22 Jan. 1779; 27 Mch. 1782.
Sons James and Alvin; my seven children Job, James, Alvin, Mary, Joseph,
Jonas and Peggy.

MUSE, EDWARD, Snr., 14 Nov. 1781; 30 Apl. 1782.
Wife Ann; son Edward; grandchildren Sanford and Thomas sons of William
Muse; grandson Edward son of Edward Muse; son George.

NEALE, DANIEL, 13 Sept. 1781; 30 Apl. 1782.
Son Presley; daughters Nancy and Mary Neale; son Peter Presley Neale;
son James; daughter Elizabeth Neale; wife Dorcas.

JENKINS, RICHARD, 2 Feb. 1782; 28 May 1782.
Sons William and Richard; dau. Jemima Barker; dau. Frances Jenkins; son
Joseph; son Thomas; son Presley; dau. Sabina Jenkins; son Smith Jenkins;
wife Sabella; son John Barker Jenkins; son Daniel.

ANTON, ALEXANDER, 27 Apl. 1782; 28 May 1782.
Daughters Mary, Elizabeth and Ann; son Robert.

MUSE, JANE, 9 May 1782; 25 June 1782.
Granddaughters Jane and Anne Carmichael; dau. Jane Edrington; dau. Patty
Price; dau. Catherine Strother; grandson Daniel Carmichael; exor. Christo-
pher Edrington.

PIERCE, WILLIAM, 2 Dec. 1781; 25 June 1782.
My wife; dau. Batty; dau. Jane Triplett; grandson William; son John Lovell
and dau. Molly.

DOZIER, WILLIAM, 18 July 1782; 30 July 1782.
Sons Richard, James Smith and William Robinson Dozier; daughters Elizabeth Porter, Ann Robinson Porter, Martha Packett and Jemima Redman.

COLLINSWORTH, WILLOUGHBY, 9 May 1782; 30 July 1782.
Son John the land I bought of John Collingworth; my three daus. Sarah,
Ann and Jean; wife Sarah; Vincent Collingworth.

SCOTT, THOMAS, 31 Jan. 1782; 24 Sept. 1782.
Wife Sarah; daughter Elizabeth; son Charles and all my children; brother Charles Scott.

SMITH, WILLIAM, 14 May 1782; 26 Nov. 1782.
Son Francis William Smith; son Benjamin Pope Smith; dau. Mary Smith; dau. Rachel Muse; children William Windsor, Benjamin Pope and Mary Smith; sister Anne Smith; wife Susetta.

BAILEY, WILLIAM, 20 April 1779; 26 Nov. 1782.
Wife Mary Bailey; brother Daniel Bailey; brother John Bailey.

ROBINSON, WILLIAM, gent., 3 Aug. 1782; 25 Feb. 1782.
My son; to each of my daughters when 21.

LOWE, RICHARD, 4 Oct. 1782; 25 Feb. 1783.
Son Richard; daughter Elizabeth.

REDMAN, SOLOMON, 31 Jan. 1783; 25 Feb. 1783.
To Miss Ann Weeks; William Redman Kelsick and Ann Kelsick; son Henry S. Redman; grandson Solomon Redman Sanford; dau. Sally; dau. Winifred Sanford; to Sarah Redman; daughter Kelsick's children.

CANNADAY, JAMES, 8 Aug. 1782; 25 Mch. 1783.
Wife Ann; dau. Susannah Cannaday; son Reuben.

JACKSON, SAMUEL, 14 Dec. 1782; 25 Mch. 1783.
Wife Jean Johnson alias Jackson; children William Barnard, Sarah, George, Nancy and Johnson Jackson.

HUTT, JOHN, 13 Nov. 1782; 25 Mch. 1783.
Brother William; brother Gerrard R.; sister Betty R. Hutt; goddau. Sarah Lawson.

CRABB, VINCENT, 8 Feb. 1782; 29 Apl. 1783.
Wife Jemima; son John; brother Gerrard Crabb; dau. Sarah Crabb.

CLAYTOR, WILLIAM, 21 Feb. 1783; 29 Apl. 1783.
Mary wife of James Starks; to Brookes Mothershead; to Elizabeth Starks; to Joshua Hinson land in Richmond co.; Ann wife of Peter Self.

WEAVER, BENJAMIN, 1 July 1782; 29 Apl. 1783.
Son John; dau. Sukey Weaver; daughters Sabinah, Ailsey and Fanny Weaver; son Daniel; brother John Weaver.

BAYNES, JOHN, 22 Feb. 1783; 29 Apl. 1783.
To Betty S. Connoly; brother Mathew Baynes.

MARTIN, JOHN, 3 Nov. 1780; Codicil 14 Feb. 1781; 29 Apl. 1783.
Wife Mary Ann; dau. Sarah Martin; dau. Charity McKettrick; son Jacob.

PORTER, DANIEL, 8 Sept. 1781; 28 Oct. 1783.
Son Benjamin; to William Dozier Porter, John Porter and Ned Porter; wife Elizabeth.

TURNBULL, STEPHEN, 1 Nov. 1783; 30 Mch. 1784.
My wife decd.; children Margaret, Elizabeth, James, George and Reuben.

BERRYMAN, WILLIAM, 21 Aug. 1783; 30 Mch. 1784.
Eldest son Benjamin; grandsons Willoughby Newton and Henry Eskridge Berryman sons of Benjamin Berryman; Mrs. Rose Grigsby of Stafford; sons Newton, John, Thomas, Gerrard; daughters Winifred and Elizabeth; to son Newton silver spoons with the crest of the Newtons on their handles; sons Waters, Gerrard, Thomas, Francis and Josias.

SANFORD, WILLIAM, 31 May 1782; 30 Mch. 1784.
Children Charles, Richard, William, Jeremiah; daughters Mary Bulger and Sarah Marmaduke; wife Barbara.

HARRISON, SAMUEL, ———; 27 Apl. 1784.
Son Peter; dau. Elsey Harrison; to Thomas Harrison; to Hannah Harrison.

WEEKS, BENJAMIN, 2 Dec. 1782; 27 Apl. 1784.
Grandson Benjamin Pope Smith; grandson Benjamin son of my son Charles Weekes Steel; dau. Susetta Smith; dau. Mary Weekes Steel; dau. Selia Weeks.

STEPTOE, DR. GEORGE, 22 Jan. 1783; 27 May 1784.
The child my wife Elizabeth goes with; son Edward; brothers James and William Steptoe.

MULLINS, PETER, 23 June 1780; 25 May 1784.
To wife Elizabeth.

DOLMAN, WILLIAM, 31 July 1783; 25 May 1784.
Two sons John Henry and William; daughters Betsy and Peggy Dolman; wife Mary.

DRAKE, SARAH, 5 Feb. 1784; 29 June 1784.
Son Benjamin.

MEEKS, ANN, 1 Apl. 1784; 27 July 1784.
To Winny Sanford; to Ann Y. Kelsick; to Henry S. Redman; to William Redman Kelsick; sister Sarah Smith; sister Elizabeth Porter; sister Judith Nash; niece Ann Meeks Packett; to Lawrence Waddey Sanford.

McKENNEY, JOHN, Snr., 12 May 1784; 31 Aug. 1784.
Sons Duke and Joseph; daughter Barbara Monroe; wife Nelly.

JEFFRIES, ROBERT, 28 Feb. 1784; 30 Nov. 1784.
Wife Mary; to John Elinore and daughter Catherine Elinore; sons Robert, Jeremiah and James.

MUSE, JAMES, 20 July 1784; 30 Nov. 1784.
Wife Susanna; son Charles; son Lawrence; friends Hudson Muse and Daniel Muse of Northumberland exors.

WEAVER, JOHN, 28 July 1783; 30 Nov. 1784.
Brother Zachariah Weaver; to Elizabeth Bayn; to John son of Benjamin Weaver; brother Abraham Weaver; to Robert Moxley; to Daniel Weaver; to Joseph Moxley, Jr.; wife Sarah.

MONROE, GEORGE, 7 Nov. 1775; 24 Sept. 1776.
Son William; dau. Sarah Kitchen; granddaughter Sally Kitchen; son John; daughters Elizabeth, Mary and Molly; sons Andrew and John; dau. in law Elizabeth Monroe; granddaughters Ann and Elizabeth Monroe; son William exor.

PAYTON, JOHN, 13 Mch. 1774; 30 June 1778.
Sons John, William, Wharton and Thomas Payton.

MUSE, NICHOLAS, 4 May 1778; 30 Mch. 1779.
Wife Elizabeth; sons Jeremiah, Walker and Jesse; daughters Penelope Muse, Elizabeth Washington, Mary Randall and Ann Washington; brother Daniel Muse.

ROBINSON, HARRY, 22 Sept. 1777; 29 Sept. 1778.
My mother to have land in King George; to William and Alice Robinson children of my brother William Robinson.

COURTNEY, LEONARD, Snr., 28 July 1780; 28 Nov. 1780.
To sons James and Leonard lands in Fauquier; younger sons William and George; wife Kezia; daughter Peggy Courtney; grandson Samuel Courtney; daughter Sally Turner; daughter Mary.

CHANDLER, ELIZABETH, ———; 28 Mch. 1780.
To daughter Jane Chandler all estate.

McKENNY, VINCENT, 9 Oct. 1779; 28 Mch. 1780.
Wife Ann and sons and daughters; son Rodham.

JACKSON, WILLIAM, Snr., 2 June 1780; 25 July 1780.
Sister Elizabeth Franklin; to William Franklin; to Jane Nash.

DRAKE, RICHARD, of King George; 30 Aug. 1760; 25 July 1780.
Son William; son in law John Green; wife Frances and my eight children and the one she is now great with, viz: Elizabeth, Sarah, Elenor, Thomas, James, Sukey, John and Richard; cousin Thomas Drake.

KITCHEN, SARAH, 19 Oct. 1780; 31 Oct. 1780.
To daughter Sally Kitchen; brother William Monroe exor.

CARTER, JANE, 15 Feb. 1781; 27 Feb. 1781.
Son James Carpenter; son John Carpenter; to James Nash; dau. Anne Carpenter; son William Carter; dau. Elizabeth Carter.

GRIGGS, WILLIAM, 18 Apl. 1778; 31 July 1781.
My second son William when 21; wife Mary and all my children; son John.

COLLINGSWORTH, JOHN, Snr., 17 May 1781; 28 Aug. 1781.
Sons William and Nathaniel; father in law Nathaniel Butler and brother in law William Smith exors.

RUST, PETER, 6 Mch. 1781; 26 Mch. 1782.
Sons Samuel and Peter and youngest son Jeremiah; my seven daughters Elizabeth, Jane, Charlotte, Mary Sophia, Harriett, Lucinda and Caroline; my wife Rebecca; exor. John Rust.

SANFORD, AUGUSTINE, 30 May 1785; 25 Oct. 1785.
Wife Henrietta; to son Robert land from my uncle John Sanford's estate; sons Richard and Thomas Randall Sanford; son Augustine; dau. Mary Thorn; dau. Elizabeth Gilbert otherwise Rust.

SANFORD, WILLOUGHBY, 5 Dec. 1785; 28 Nov. 1786.
Daughter Ann Templeman; dau. Elizabeth Barnett; dau. Mary Butler Harrison; son John at 21.

BRINNON, JOHN, ———; 30 June 1778.
Wife Hannah; dau. Ann Crenshaw; grandchildren Hannah and Ann Rice; dau. Hannah Holland; sons John and George; dau. Elizabeth Brinnon.

SANFORD, JOHN, 1 Oct. 1776; 27 Oct. 1778.
Four grandchildren Francis Sanford, Jemima Spence, Molly Harrison and Butler Sanford; son Willoughby; son in law Thomas Sanford and my daughter Jemima Sanford exors.

SORRELL, JUDITH, 6 Feb. 1786; 28 Feb. 1786.
Sons Thomas and James.

GORDON, GEORGE, 8 Oct. 1784; 28 Feb. 1786.
Wife Ursula; son George; son John lands at Sheepbridge, Lisduff, etc., in Co. of Down, Ireland; daughters Hannah and Betty Gordon arrears of rent due me from Mr. Samuel Gordon, merchant in Ireland.

RUST, JOHN, 7 Sept. 1785; 28 Feb. 1786.
Wife Jane; children John, Elizabeth, Jane and Molly Rust; brother Peter Rust.

FITZHUGH, DANIEL, 17 Sept. 1777; 28 Mch. 1786.
To be buried in my brother William's burying yard; son William; daughters Jane and Sukey; my brother William's children by his wife Hannah; niece Lucy Fitzhugh and niece Ann daughters of my brother William; friend William Fitzhugh of Chatham; my decd. wife Susanna.

MONROE, JEMIMA, 2 Dec. 1785; 25 Apl. 1786.
Daughter Elizabeth Monroe; son William; exor. Mr. Benjamin Monroe.

HIPKINS, RICHARD, 17 Mch. 1786; 25 April 1786.
Son Robert Spottswood Hipkins at 21; sons Thomas and William Augustus; daughters Mary, Elizabeth and Charlotte Hipkins; son Thomas; my wife.

HARRISON, MAGDALENE, 16 Dec. 1775; 27 June 1786.
Son Jeremiah; dau. Hannah Gilbert; my husband Samuel Harrison decd.

SANFORD, EDWARD, 25 Dec. 1785; 25 July 1786.
Wife Catherine alias Pope; son Patrick; son Edward Sanford alias Pope; daughter Jemima Stone; dau. Susannah Sanford; son Robert Sanford alias Pope; son Richard Sanford alias Pope; daughters Elizabeth and Caty Sanford Pope; granddaughter Elizabeth Spence Sutton.

BAILEY, DANIEL, 17 Oct. 1785; 30 Nov. 1786.
Brothers John, Samuel and Vincent Smith Bailey.

BRICKEY, PETER, 16 Sept. 1786; 27 Feb. 1787.

Wife Winifred; sons Gerard, John, Peter and William; grandson Peter son of Gerard; grandson Gerard son of John; grandchildren John and Nancy Kirkham; granddaughter Winney Lucas Garner; my daughters Temperance Morgan, Dorcas Garner, Winifred Kirkham and Ann Sanford.

BEALE, THOMAS, 10 Jan. 1786; 26 June 1787.

Wife Elizabeth; son William; daughters Alice Rust, Massey, Brand and Elizabeth Olive; son Samuel.

SMITH, WILLIAM, 8 Sept. 1784; 28 Nov. 1786.

Wife Hannah; son Samuel and the rest of my children.

WASHINGTON, JOHN, 3 July 1785; 26 June 1787.

Wife Constant and all my children, Sarah Harper excepted; the child my wife is big with; to son William Henry my seal with the family arms on it; son Thomas Lund Washington; son Robert Townsend Washington decd.; my seven children, John Terrett, William Henry, Thomas Lund, Robert Pitt, George, Louisa F., Nancy Constantia and the child my wife goes with; exors. William Fitzhugh of Chatham and my nephew Henry Washington.

LACY, JOSEPH, 13 Feb. 1785; 25 Sept. 1787.

Daughter Margaret Lacy; wife Jane and my children.

MASSEY, LOVEL, 22 Nov. 1777; 30 June 1778.

Land given me by my father where my mother now lives to my daughters Sukey and Patty Massey; my wife extx.

QUESENBERRY, ELIZABETH, 23 May 1784; 22 Feb. 1785.

To Elijah son of William Weaver; to Richard Weaver son of the same; to William and Nicholas Dodd; to Ann Weaver and her eldest daughter Elizabeth Bayn; to John and William Quesenberry.

MIDDLETON, BENEDICT, 29 May 1782; 27 Sept. 1785.

Wife Hannah; grandson Benedict Lamkin; my five daughters Elizabeth Lewis, Jane Wroe, Hannah, Martha and Ann Middleton; to dau. Elizabeth Lewis and the children she had by her first husband Francis Wright, and the child she has or may have by her present husband Mr. George Lewis; extx. my wife; brother in law Col. Joseph Lane; nephew Capt. William Middleton.

MORGAN, DANIEL, 20 Sept. 1782; 26 Aug. 1789.

My wife; to Daniel son of my brother David Morgan; my brothers William, Andrew and Benjamin Morgan.

CRABB JANE, 19 Dec. 1773; 30 Oct. 1781.

Son Gerard; grandson Abraham Garner; son Vincent; daughter Sukey Garner; son Osmund.

FRESHWATER, GEORGE, 14 Dec. 1779; 25 Apl. 1780.

Daughters Mary, Elizabeth, Ann and Sarah Freshwater; wife Elenor; son Thomas.

JETT, CATHERINE, 7 Nov. 1786; 27 Feb. 1787.
Mentions land in King George county; daughters Betty and Frances Jett; dau. Ann Brown; exor. Peter Jett.

RANSDELL, EDWARD, 19 June 1773; 30 Nov. 1773.
Wife Elizabeth; dau. Elizabeth and her husband James Davenport; to Mr. Richard Parker; nephew Presley son of my brother Wharton Ransdell; nephew Edward son of my brother William Ransdell.

TIDWELL, ANN B., 20 Oct. 1784; 28 Mch. 1786.
Three daughters Hannah and Barbara Tidwell and Betty Muse; son Joseph Sanford; dau. Beckey Dozier and her daughter Sarah Dozier; exors. Thomas Muse and Richard Dozier.

SMITH, PETER, Snr., 1 Apl. 1774; ———— Aug. 1774.
Sons John, Peter, William; grandson Peter Smith; dau. Mary Holloway; dau. Dorcas Neale; grandchildren William and Elizabeth Turner.

BOOK XVIII.

WASHINGTON, JOHN AUGUSTINE, 2 June 1784; Codicil 19 Nov. 1785; 31 July 1787.
Wife Hannah; son Bushrod; son Corbin land in Loudoun; daughter Jenny Washington and my son in law William Washington; granddaughter Ann Aylett Washington; dau. Mildred Washington the land conveyed by my mother Mrs. Mary Washington and the land I bought of Robert Washington; wife Hannah, my esteemed brother General Washington and my sons Richard Bushrod and Corbin exors.

WASHINGTON, WILLIAM, 2 Mch. 1786; 25 Mch. 1788.
Niece Peggy Buckner; brother John Washington; nephews John Hooe Washington and Richard Henry Buckner.

TURNER, THOMAS, 2 June 1787; 30 Oct. 1787.
Wife Jane; dau. Elizabeth Cock; dau. Jean Turner; youngest dau. Mary Turner; eldest son Harry Smith Turner; sons Thomas, George and Richard, the latter to have plantation at Port Royal.

DRAKE, BENJAMIN, 1 Mch. 1788; 29 Apl. 1788.
To cousin Jessy Green all my estate.

OMOHUNDRO, THOMAS, 14 Apl. 1788; 29 July 1788.
Daughter Ann Moxley and her dau. Molly Moxley; sons Thomas, William, Bruce and Richard; wife Martha; dau. Martha Omohundro.

GILBERT, WILLIAM, 16 Feb. 1785; 29 July 1788.
Wife Hannah and the child she goes with; son William; children Nancy Gilbert and Samuel Gilbert (child whose name cannot be made out).

CARTER, ANN, 5 Jan. 1789; 31 Mch. 1789.
Sons Robert, Samuel, John and George; daughters Ann Annadale, Sarah Payne, Mary Neale, Frances, Jane and Lucy Carter; sons Presley and Richard; exors. son in law Presley Neale and Daniel McCarty.

GILBERT, MARTHA, 7 Aug. 1775; 28 July 1789.
Sister Mary; to Ann Smith; brother in law William Morton.

BENNETT, THOMAS, 15 Oct. 1787; 25 Aug. 1789.
Estate to son Richard.

MIDDLETON, JOHN, 3 Jan. 1789; 25 Aug. 1789.
Wife Martha; son Jeremiah at 21; dau. Sally Middleton; friend George Middleton exor.

SMITH, THOMAS, Rector of Cople, 14 Dec. 1788; 27 Oct. 1789.
Sons Thomas Gregory and John Augustine at 21; wife Mary; dau. Sarah; to Mr. Philip Lee who married my daughter Mary; godson Baldwin Mathews Lee; brother Col. Gregory Smith.

SMITH, JACOB, 20 May 1789; 27 Oct. 1789.
Son Henry; children Francis, Henry and Jacob; wife Ann.

PAYNE, GEORGE, 6 Apl. 1787; 26 Jan. 1790.
Brother Richard Payne decd.; sons William, George and John; dau. Jane Kelly; dau. Mary Morris; brother Daniel Payne.

BRISCOE, DANIEL, town of Leeds, 2 Apl. 1789; 27 Apl. 1790.
Son John; daughters Elizabeth, Ellen, Martha and Lucy; wife Elizabeth and brother Reuben exors.

SHOATS, GEORGE, 8 Apl. 1790; 25 May 1790.
Daughter Mary Butler; daughter Elizabeth Shoats.

JETT, JOHN, 2 Mch. 1790; 29 June 1790.
Son Burkett; son Newton; daughter Ann Jett; wife Isabel.

OMOHUNDRO, JAMES, 31 Oct. 1788; 27 July 1790.
Sons James, Richard and William; dau. Ann; wife Elizabeth.

COLLINSWORTH, SARAH, 23 May 1790; 28 Dec. 1790.
To John Collinsworth the land left me by my father; to William Steel and then to Thomas son of William Franklin.

MIDDLETON, WILLIAM, 26 June 1790; 25 Jan. 1791.
Son Robert; son William land in Northumberland; son John land in Northumberland; my three daughters Elizabeth, Mary Fleet Middleton and Hannah Middleton.

ATWELL, JOHN, 24 Nov. 1790; 25 Jan. 1791.
Nephew John son of my brother Francis; brother William Atwell; to Elizabeth Humes; my brother Youell Atwell's estate; sister Martha Sorrell; to William Redman, Jr.

DOZIER, RICHARD, 12 Jan. 1786; 30 May 1791.
James son of Richard Dozier, Jr.; nephew Joseph Dozier; nephew Thomas Dozier; niece Betty Walker Dozier.

MUSE, GEORGE, 3 May 1791; 2 June 1791.
Daughter Ann Sanford Hall; daughters Peggy and Elizabeth Muse; son George; five small children Burkett, Franky, Rebecca, Elenor and George; friends Richard Muse and Newman Hall exors.

COX, FLEET, 7 Jan. 1791; 28 June 1791.
Sons Peter Presley, Fleet, John, James and Richard Cox; dau. Molly Middleton; dau. Betty Downing; son in law Thomas Downing.

PAYTON, GEORGE C., 12 Nov. 1790; 28 June 1791.
Brother Anthony Payton; sister Ann Drake; sister Elizabeth Butler.

CLARK, MARGARET, 23 Nov. 1790; 28 June 1791.
Son William Morton Clark; brother and sister James and Hannah Morton; exor. father William Morton.

PAYTON, WILLIAM, 14 Mch. 1791; 25 Oct. 1791.
Wife Mary; son James and all my children.

JETT, WILLIAM, 21 June 1791; 25 Oct. 1791.
Daughter Peggy Jett Bartlett; exor. Anthony Payton.

MUSE, ELIZABETH, 23 May 1791; 29 Nov. 1791.
Son Jeremiah; dau. Penelope Muse; granddaughter Betsy Muse; son Walker Muse.

MUSE, MARY, 26 Oct. 1790; 28 Feb. 1792.
Niece Susannah Muse; sister in law Elizabeth Muse; nephew Elliott Muse; brothers James, Thomas and Nicholas Muse.

STURMAN, ELLIOTT, 26 Feb. 1791; 4 Mch. 1792.
Wife Mary; sons William Young and Foxhall Sturman, latter when 21; nephew Elliott Muse and Richard Elliott Parker.

WRIGHT, FRANCIS, 5 Dec. 1775; 26 Mch. 1793.
Three sons Bernard, Johnson and Wright Wright; wife Elizabeth.

MIDDLETON, GEORGE, 26 Apl. 1793; 30 July 1793.
Godson George M. Wright; to Elizabeth widow of Jeremiah Rust; all estate left me by my father to Jeremiah Middleton; to Malinda M. Bennett; to Thomas, Mary, Elizabeth, Sarah and Martha Rust the children of Jeremiah Rust decd.

MORTON, WILLIAM, 11 July 1793; 30 July 1793.
Wife Ann; son James; grandson William Morton Clark; dau. Hannah Morton.

SANFORD, YOUELL, 16 Nov. 1793; 28 Jan. 1794.
Sister Elenor Sanford and then to her son Robert; sons Daniel and William Sanford; daughters Barbara, Caty, Peggy, Jemima, Malinda and Frances; son Thomas; my wife.

TEMPLEMAN, THOMAS, 8 Sept. 1793; 25 Feb. 1794.
Son Samuel; son Thomas; daughters Molly and Fanny Templeman; brother Samuel Templeman and his wife Ann exors.

HARVEY, MUNGO, 8 Feb. 1794; 29 Apl. 1794.
Sons James and John; three daughters Ann, Sarah and Elizabeth; my **wife**.

WESTMORELAND COUNTY MILITIA.

ORDER BOOKS.

Court 25 March 1777.
Lewis Smith to be Ensign in Capt. William Nelson's company.
John Richards qualified as Captain of a company of militia.
Thomas Yeatman, Lieut., and Edward Muse as Ensign in Capt. James Muse's company.
Court 29 July 1777.
The oath of allegiance to be administered within the following districts:
Captain Jacob Martin's militia company.
Captain Peter Jett's
Captain William Nelson's
Captain James Muse's
Captain Thomas Chilton's
Captain John Rice's
Captain John Rochester's
Captain Daniel Morgan's
Court 26 Aug. 1777.
Jeremiah Garland to be 2nd Lieut., and Richard Atwell, Ensign, in Captain Daniel Morgan's company.
William Middleton, 1st Lieut., and Fleet Cox., Jnr., as 2nd Lieut., in Captain John Rochester's company.
John Turberville, 2nd Lieut., and George Fairfax Lee, Ensign in Captain John Rice's company.
William Edwards, 1st Lieut., William Brown, 2nd Lieut., and Daniel McKenney, Ensign, in Captain Joseph Lane's company.
Patrick Sanford as 2nd Lieut., and Edward Sanford, Jr., Ensign, in Captain Thomas Chilton's company.
George Robinson as 2nd Lieut. to Captain James Muse's company.
George Berkely as 2nd Lieut. to Capt. William Nelson's company.
Benjamin Monroe as 2nd Lieut. to Captain Peter Jett's company.
Christopher Edrington as 2nd Lieut. to Captain Jacob Martin's company.
Court 25 Nov. 1777.
Richard Atwell, gent., 2nd Lieut. in Captain Daniel Morgan's company.
William Edwards, gent., 1st Lieut. in Capt. Joseph Lane's company.
William Brown, gent., 2nd Lieut. in Capt. Joseph Lane's company.
Court 26 May 1778.
For forming a company of militia taken into this county from the county of King George, the officers for the said company are:
James Tripplett, Captain; John Edrington, 1st Lieut.; Richard Sanford, 2nd Lieut., and William Marshall, Ensign.
Thomas Chilton, gent., is recommended for Lieut.-Colonel.
Joseph Lane, gent., is recommended for Major.

John Berkley, 1st Lieut., Lewis Smith, 2nd Lieut., and Beckwith Butler, Ensign to Captain William Nelson's company.

Patrick Sanford, 1st Lieut., Edward Sanford, 2nd Lieut., and Vincent Marmaduke, Ensign to Captain Thomas Chilton's company.

Court 28 July 1778.

The following confirmations were made by His Excellency the Governor:

Thomas Chilton, Lieut.-Colonel; John Lane, Major; James Triplett, Captain.

Court 25 Aug. 1778.

Richard Sanford commissioned as 2nd Lieut. in Capt. Triplett's company.

Court 23 Feb. 1779.

The following gentlemen produced their commissions and took the oath:

Patrick Sanford, Captain; Edward Sanford, 1st Lieut.; Vincent Marmaduke, 2nd Lieut.; Thomas Spence, Ensign.

William Edwards recommended as Captain of militia for the company formerly commanded by Major Joseph Lane.

Court 29 June 1779.

William Edwards, gent., appointed Captain of the company formerly commanded by Major Joseph Lane.

John Berkeley, gent., produced his commission appointing him 1st Lieut. to Captain William Nelson's company.

Court 27 July 1779.

Recommended to His Excellency the Governor, Daniel McKinney, 1st Lieut.; William Robinson Dozier, 2nd Lieut.; Garland Moore, Ensign, all to Captain William Edwards' company.

Lewis Smith presented a commission of the Governor bearing date 26 May last, as 2nd Lieut. in Captain William Nelson's company.

Court 31 Jan. 1781.

Robert Harper is recommended for Captain of the company formerly commanded by Captain James Triplett.

William Storke Jett, 1st Lieut.; John Hungerford, 2nd Lieut., and Charles Deane, Ensign, are recommended to Captain Harper's company of militia.

Court 24 April 1781.

The following are recommended to the Governor:

Joseph Lane, gent., for Lieut.-Colonel of this county in place of Col. Thomas Chilton, decd.; William Nelson as Major in room of Joseph Lane; Elliott Monroe as Captain in room of William Nelson; Samuel Kemp as Ensign in Captain John Rice's company in the room of George Fairfax Lee who has resigned.

Court 29 May 1781.

Recommended to the Governor:

William Parker as Captain; John Chilton as Lieutenant; Henry Washington as Ensign.

John Brinnon is appointed 1st Lieutenant to Captain John Rice's company of militia in the room of John Simpson who hath resigned he being engaged in the cavalry.

Court 28 Aug. 1781.

John Bailey, Ensign in Captain John Rochester's company of militia, resigns his commission and Christopher Collins is recommended to the Governor for the vacancy.

WESTMORELAND COUNTY LAND GRANTS

DISTRICT AND COUNTY LAND GRANTS

WESTMORELAND COUNTY LAND GRANTS

Book No. 3.

Page.	Name.	Date.	No. Acres.
14	Gervase Dodson	1653	1,300
272	Vallentine Patton	1654	1,000
273	John Walton and John Bagnall	1654	3,900
275	Richard Hawkins	1654	500
275	Mrs. Margaret Brent	1654	700
276	Richard Browne	1654	200
278	Thomas Frizzar	1654	300
279	Nathaniel Pope	1654	1,000
280	Robert Yoe	1654	650
284	Richard Codsford	1654	400
284	William Robinson and Cornelius Johnson	1654	400
285	Major Miles Cary	1654	3,000
297	David Mansell	1654	600
299	William Beach	1654	700
301	Thomas Fowke	1654	3,350
302	Humphrey Higgenson and Abraham Moone	1654	2,000
303	Lieut.-Col. Giles Brent	1654	1,518
306	Col. John Matrom	1654	3,609
308	Capt. Giles Brent	1654	300
312	Nicholas Marteaw	1654	2,000
313	Robert Hubard	1654	1,600
319	Mrs. Francis Harrison	1654	1,600
325	Richard Browne	1654	650
328	Christopher Boor	1654	300
328	Edward Parker	1654	300
329	Ann Bernard	1654	1,500
356	George Wall	1655	1,200
357	William Gooch and Robert Vauly	1655	6,000
363	Nicholas Marteaw	1655	2,000

363	Thomas Wilsford 1655	50
364	Richard Codsford 1655	400
363	John Withers 1655	150
373	John Withers 1654	1,000
373	Mr. Giles Brent 1654	1,000
374	Francis Smith, Ingeenr., and John Smith, of Stanly Hundred......1654	3,000
376	Nicholas Merywether 1654	3,000
376	Same 1654	1,350
391	David Philips 1656	400
391	John Harrison 1655	1,000

Book No. 4.

7	Robert Vaulx 1655	6,000
18	William Botham 1655	500
23	Richard Coale and David Anderson 1655	150
51	Nathaniel Pope 1656	1,550
59	John Lear 1655	100
63	Lieut.-Col. Nathaniel Pope 1656	1,505
75	John Rosier, clarke 1656	1,050
84	Herbert Smith 1656	500
98	Margaret Miles 1656	1,200
99	Robert Hubbard and William Lewis 1656	2,000
103	Robert Hubbard 1654	500
103	Robert Hubbard 1654	500
125	Thomas Graves 1656	300
133	Mrs. Mary Brent 1657	1,250
134	Henry Footman ....blank	300
134	Giles Brent 1657	1,340
173	John Wood 1657	500
175	William Thomas 1657	1,000
183	Lieut.-Col. Miles Cary 1657	3,000
191	George Seaton 1657	300
210	Capt. Ed. Streater ....,.......1657	3,000
220	Richard Hubord 1657	250
230	John Bennett 1658	150
234	William Martin 1657	1,000
241	Anthony Stephens 1657	850
255	Henry Payton 1657	400
257	Robert Vauly 1657	2,000
262	Henry Roach 1657	140
262	John Bennett 1658	210

263	Richard Searle and William Spence	1658	60
265	John Lewis and Robert Joanes	1658	2,000
270	John Williams and Stephen Norman	1657	1,200
279	Maj. James Goodwin	1657	1,000
281	John Drayton	1657	2,000
283	William Strowder	1658	500
284	David Phillips	1657	350
286	Richard Searle	1657	550
293	Lieut.-Col. Nathaniel Pope	1657	1,500
294	Gervase Dodson	1657	5,200
305	Richard Wright	1658	2,200
306	Christopher Harris	1658	2,000
309	Charles Ashton	1658	400
312	Capt Peter Ashton	1658	2,000
316	William and John Heabord	1658	300
318	Richard Wells	1658	100
324	Henry Roach	1658	1,700
337	Gravase Dodson	1658	600
338	Mr. John Ellis	1658	1,400
338	John Evans	1658	1,650
341	Maj. James Goodwin	1658	400
342	John Withers	1658	320
342	William Withers	1658	400
353	John Curtis	1657	1,300
369	John Maddison	1658	300
371	Col. Thomas Pettus	1658	1,000
371	Col. George Read	1657	2,000
383	John Dodman	1662	350
417	Giles Brent, Jr.	1662	1,800
421	Arthur Shore and Henry Cossum	1662	350
426	Valentine Payton	1662	1,600
430	Richard Browne	1662	300
434	Isaac Allerton	1662	500
441	Giles Brent	1662	1,000
446	William Drummond	1661	4,750
447	Col. Richard Lee	166-	4,000
450	Richard Bushrod	1660	2,000
456	Peter Ashton	1661	2,550
492	William Overed	1661	400
550	Walter Broadhurst	1662	300
553	Gerrard Broadhurst	1662	500
555	Katherine Brent	1662	1,050

555	William Hallows	1662	3,900
571	Henry Vincent	1662	550
611	George Wading	1664	600
612	Thomas Butler	1664	391
623	William Struder	1664	500

Book No. 5.

14	Richard Bushrod	1662	2,000
36	Anthony Arnold	1665	500
36	John Alexander	1664	550
37	John Beard	1664	245
37	John and Thomas Palmer	1664	365
38	Maj. John Washington	1664	320
41	Robt. Alexander, John Alexander, Jr., and Christopher Alexander	1664	1,460
41	George Weading	1664	212
42	Thomas Pope	1664	2,454
49	John Washington	1664	300
45	Alexander Benum	1664	257
49	Maj. John Washington and Thomas Pope	1661	50
52	Ann Pope, alias Washington	1661	700
53	William Court and Robert Hutcheson	1662	660
54	John Washington and Thomas Pope	1661	1,200
55	Dorothy Brooks alias Butler	1664	650
120	Robert Selfe	1665	300
129	Richard Griffin	1664	57
141	Vincent Coe	1665	400
142	John Rosier	1662	1,450
148	William Tilt	1662	400
149	Giles Brent	1662	1,000
151	Mary Pate	1662	300
153	Thomas Humphries and Thomas Tupper	1662	547
154	Vincent Young	1662	200
154	James Harris	1662	60
158	John and Thomas Buckocks	1662	350
160	William Brown, Danl. White and Wm. Baltrop	1662	745
169	Wm. and John Heaberd	1662	350
171	Richard Heaberd	1662	480
171	Henry Brookes	1662	1,020

173	Sarah, Margaret, Judith and Elizabeth Jones 1662	100
173	William Green 1662	250
174	John Drayton 1662	2,000
214	Christopher Booze 1662	300
215	Wm. Heaberd and Wm. Horton...1663	1,600
220	John Butler 1663	350
224	Francis Gray 1663	374
224	Capt. John Ashton 1663	783
224	Same 1663	543
225	John Frissell 1663	104
227	Christopher Butler 1663	150
227	John Lord and Wm. Horton......1663	2,500
228	John Butler 1663	160
239	Lt. Col. Giles Brent 1662	1,518
239	Daniel Wild, and Francis Kirkman 1663	2,000
240	Margaret Brent 1662	700
244	Daniel White 1661	69
250	William Freeke 1662	600
260	Gerard Fowke 1662	3,650
261	Col. Valentine Payton 1662	650
263	Andrew Pettigrew 1662	5,200
265	John Matron 1662	3,609
275	Richard Sturman 1664	2,000
276	Henry Vincent 1664	400
290	Henry Payton 1664	1,000
296	Samuel Hayward 1662	200
299	Robert Vauly 1662	6,000
312	Isaac Watson and Samuel Mottershead 1663	400
327	Thomas Wilsford 1662	50
353	Charles Wood 1663	268
373	James Pope 1662	1,000
393	Thomas Dios 1664	500
394	Same 1664	1,200
415	Thomas Phillpot 1664	500
421	William Horton 1663	600
440	John Bruerton 1664	1,456
441	William Hardick 1664	1,000
484	Wilkes Maunder 1665	1,000
494	Col. Peter Ashton 1665	500
495	Edward Rogers 1665	600
498	Nicholas Jarnew 1665	178

499	Samuel Bonam	1665	99
521	Raleigh Traverse	1665	3,659
523	James Harris	1665	60
525	Stephen Warman	1663	750
530	John Lord	1662	1,200
531	Christopher Butler	1662	123¾
532	Wm. Horton	1665	100
545	John Lord	1664	100
578	John Whetstone	1665	250
578	Ralph and Thomas Blag	1665	209
579	Wm. Overett and George Browne	1665	400
579	Randolph Kirke	1665	1,000
580	Wm. Basely and Ed. Haelly	1665	1,000
580	James Green, Francis Lewis and Wm. Baldrop	1665	1,050
581	Richard Stereman	1665	2,000
582	Wm. Overett	1665	590
583	Wm. Pearce	1665	1,810
590	Robt. Alexander and George Weeding	1665	800
632	Thomas Greg	1662	450
645	Daniel Hutt	1666	875
645	Andrew Read	1666	400
646	Same	1666	400
652	Capt. Giles Brent	1666	1,000
654	Robert Middleton	1665	700

Book No. 6.

1	(Blank)	1666	60
2	Richard Heaberd	1666	1,500
11	Robert Middleton	1666	1,120
12	Francis Clay	1666	1,480
15	Richard Sturman	1666	1,004
16	John Beard	1666	250
49	Maj. Wm. Perrie	1666	4,310
50	Wm. Loyd and John Biddle	1667	4,750
55	John Whetstone, Thomas Dyar, and Patrick Spenson	1667	1,050
56	John Whetstone	1667	2,430
68	Vincent Coy	1667	665
75	Capt. John Lord	1667	1,667
76	John Lord and Wm. Horton	1667	1,544
76	Wm. Smith	1667	590

107	Ann Brett	1667	300
125	Henry Cossum	1668	450
152	James Hawley	1666	700
176	Thomas Beale a n d Randolph Kirke	1668	1,500
156	Thomas Phillpot	1668	307
179	John Withers	1668	320
179	Gerard Fowke, Wm. Horton, Richard Granger and Thomas Grigg	1661	2,000
180	Wm. Webb	1668	400
187	Col. Nicholas Spencer	1668	1,200
197	John Lee	1668	3,100
227	Maj. Wm. Pierce	1669	3,110
235	Richard Searles	1669	345
236	Same	1669	278
236	Thomas Yowell	1669	780
236	John Piper	1669	400
237	Peter Dunken	1669	140
237	Wm. Spence	1669	180
243	Wm. Browne and Wm. Baltrop	1669	744
264	Richard Coleman	1665	380
276	John Foxhall	1669	314
283	Philip Browne	1669	200
283	John Willis	1669	261
293	Mrs. Ann Barnet	1654	1,000
296	John Butler	1670	597
307	Robert Nurse	1670	189
319	Nicholas Spencer	1670	900
322	John Boocock	1670	600
324	Robert Lovell	1670	500
325	John Berriman, Wm. Horton and John Palmer	1670	1,227
327	Thomas Ludwell	1670	1,432
328	Wm. Craddock	1670	560
330	Col. Nicholas Spencer	1670	3,250
629	Elias Webb	1677	140
631	Originall Browne	1678	200
665	Malachi Peal	1678	843
671	John Quigley	1678	80
681	Adam Woffendall	1679	783
691	Daniel White	1679	600
691	George Weedon and Daniel White	1679	483

PROPRIETORS' DEEDS OR GRANTS.

Book No. 1.

14	John Spencer	1690	820
18	Ed. Hart, and Margaret, his wife	1690	880
25	Wm. Bridger	1690	700
28	Isaac Allerton	1690	284
30	Same	1690	64
33	Wm. Payne	1690	40
51	John and Thomas Collingsworth	1691	200
52	Pierce to Collingsworth		
	(Deed of Conveyance)	1682	200
64	John Rice	1691	100
84	Thomas Marson	1691	278
89	Robert Forster	1691	185
107	John Wright	1691	250
110	Thomas Mountjoy	1691	Piece of Land
112	Same	1691	
			9A.1R.29 Perches
132	Capt. Laurence Washington	1691	550
138	Mrs. Elizabeth Lord	1691	164
142	John Wright	1691	107
144	Rice Williams	1692	107
146	Martin Fisher	1692	726
154	Thomas Tanner	1692	500
158	Thomas Claiter	1692	152
162	Bunce Roe	1692	331
164	Same	1692	163
172	Susanna Adington, widow and relict of Benjamin Adington	1692	103
186	Robert Andrewes	1692	576
190	Peter Smith, Jr.	1692	70
203	Edward Frankline and Robt. Sanford	1692	413
205	Thomas Garland	1692	61
207	Nathaniel Garland	1692	205

Book No. 2.

5	George Weedon	1694	236
8	Robert Brent	1694	200
11	George Brent	1694	1,050
19	John Wheeler	1694	64
25	Robert Franke	1694	335

27	John Edwards	1694	197
29	George Thorne	1694	152
35	Meredith Edwards	1694	150
42	William Munroe	1694	60
43	Andrew Beard	1694	107
44	Saml. Baker	1694	154
46	John Fryar	1694	100
54	George Brown	1694	70
55	Same	1694	116
56	Phillip White	1694	100
57	John Davis	1694	50
74	Thomas Gulluck	1694	234
74	Isaac Allerton	1694	300
76	George Brown and Elias Marrice	1694	403
77	John Shinroe	1694	70
80	John Brown	1694	100
83	Robert Brent	1694	300
93	Edward Harris	1694	200
101	John Washington	1694	300
107	Daniel White	1694	292
125	John Nicholls	1694	163
126	Same	1694	280
171	Wm. Fitzhugh	——	475
186	Saml. Read and David Brown	1695	590
199	James Neale	1695	410
206	Richard Omohundro	1695	282
210	Benjamin Weedon and Charles Weedon	1695	169
226	Thomas Mouerly of the County of Westmoreland	1695	113
226	George Brent	1695	1,050
234	Wm. Thompson	1695	85
241	Capt. Laurence Washington	1696	5
250	Wm. Fitzhugh	1696	2,197
270	John Hartley	1697	699
271	George Harrison	1697	354
272	William Hammock	1697	161
274	Thomas Harvey	1697	220
275	John Wright Taylor	1697	229
281	Henry Kirk	1697	100
282	James Hardwick	1697	200
285	Lewis Markham	1697	100
287	John Williams	1698	28
288	John Innis Carnhill	1698	197
291	Wm. Reamy	1698	123

291	John Tucker 1698	105
298	Wm. Koherin 1698	100
303	Gilbert Croswell and John Jones...1699	139
307	Charles Smith 1699	133
309	Wm. Hammock 1699	214
310	Robert Sanford 1699	16
313	Benjamin Buryman 1699	60
317	John Gardner, Junr. 1700	200

Book No. 3.

2	John Muse, Jr. 1703	360
9	Lawrence Pope 1703	376
16	George Eskeridge 1703	58
17	Thomas Thompson 1703	63
25	Daniel Fields and Mary, his wife..1704	150
26	Same 1704	200
44	Wm. Smooth 1704	300
47	Henry Ashbury 1704	80
66	David Brown 1704	440
72	John Hudson 1704	70
73	Joshua Hudson 1704	100
74	Wm. Rush 1704	100
90	Edward Porter 1704	119
115	Robert Cole 1705	108
118	Henry Duncan 1705	197
138	Edward Ransdell 1706	141
139	George Brown 1706	215
140	Same 1706	109
141	Patrick Spence 1706	63
149	Hugh Dunahaw 1706	48
158	Elizabeth Wharton 1706	100
166	Thomas Bachellor 1707	151
169	John Wright 1707	61
171	Robert Phillips and John Muse....1707	265
178	Stephen Self 1707	100
179	Wm. Brown and Richard Sutton...1707	92
182	Capt. Daniel McCarthy 1707	151
187	Jacob Martin and Sarah his wife and the survivor of them for and during their natural lives and after their decease to descend to the heirs of John Scott 1707	220
193	Lewis Markham 1708	151½
194	Danl. Fitz Garrett and Ed. Merrick 1708	280
195	James Hewgate 1708	144

197	Anthony Carpenter	1708	164
199	Lewis Markham	1708	74
200	John Hoare	1708	20
205	Ellinor Hornebuckle	1708	200
214	Robert Ball and Gerrard Ball	1708	200
235	John Bennett and Vincent Cox	1709	765
237	John Garner	1709	180
230	Same	1709	390
240	Thomas Butler	1709	157
247	George Eskeridge	1709	305
249	Thomas Brown and George Brown	1709	130
260	Wm. Mauley	1709	216
268	John Bushrod	1710	88

Book No. 4.

7	Richard Sutton	1710	19
10	Edward Turbervile	1710	115
15	Ann Smith	1710	120
16	Same	1710	130
18	Samuel Duckiminia	1710	440
20	Burditt Ashton	1710	120
22	Wm. and John Self	1710	90
24	John Attwell	1710	475
33	Col. Richard Lee	1711	792
42	Hannah Wright	1711	71
60	Nicholas Muse	1711	179
61	St. John Shropshire	1711	33A.31 per.
74	Robert Carter, Jr.	1712	1,632
82	Stephen Latham	1712	50
84	James Byard	1712	112
86	John Chilton	1712	375
87	Thomas Sorrell	1712	127A.2R.37 per.
88	Coleman Read	1712	428
98	Capt. Gerard Hutt	1712	936
99	John Gardener	1712	17
109	Susanna Brewer	1712	105
111	Nicholas Minor	1712	296
120	Sharshall Grasty	1712	840

Book No. 5.

4	Stephen Lathom	1714	50

11	Capt. Francis Atwell	1714	114
12	Thomas Chanlor	1714	114
18	Stephen Self	1714	59A.1R.20P.
19	Charles Higginson	1716	89
32	Nathaniel Grey	1714	572
33	George Beard	1714	124
35	Susanna Brewer	1714	105
36	John Pratt, Junr.	1714	42
39	Owen Brenon	1716	155
51	Thomas Robins	1714	82
56	Wansford Arrington	1716	346
64	Same	1716	480
69	Thomas Beall	1715	140
72	John Chilton	1714	1,504
73	Richard Watts	1715	79
78	Capt Benj. Berryman	1716	27
116	Ann Smith	1715	282
117	John Williams	1715	40A.2R.20P.
123	Maj. Henry Ashton	1715	2,772
124	Christopher Butler	1716	150
127	Edward Porter	1716	70
133	Anthony Thornton	1716	123
137	Thomas Sorrell	1716	221
139	Charles Lee and Mary his wife	1713	100
144	Nicholas Minor	1715	100
157	Benj. Berryman	1717	400
172	Nicholas Minor	1718	100
180	John Awbrey	1718	140
186	John Popham	1718	100
187	Wm. Gerrard	1716	125A.2R.12P.
190	Lawrence Pope	1718	51
201	Thomas Butler	1719	200
204	Wm. Wheeler	1719	100
209	Wm. Sanders	1719	75
210	John Overhall	1715	57½
213	Thomas Russell	1719	89
215	Lawrence Butler	1719	597
222	Wm. Sturman	1719	52
226	——— Whitehouse	1719	57½
228	Jno. Garner	1719	230
232	Wm. Buttler	1719	150
238	Elias Davis	1719	49
239	Thomas Lee	1718	4,200

Book "A."

2	John Steel	1722	371
3	Daniel McCarthy	1722	21A.1R.
4	Nathaniel Gray	1722	100
5	John Ashton	1722	150
6	Christopher Butler	1722	479
35	Robert Turner	1724	107
134	Patrick Spence, Thos. Sturman, Thos. James and George Hardwitch	1724	1,678
217	John and Wm. Stuart	1726	108
226	Robert Carter, Jr.	1726	80

Book "B."

27	Robert Carter, Jr	1726	1,000
46	Maj. George Eskridge	1726	62A.80 Per.
60	Owen Brinham	1727	376
135	Willoughby Newton	1728	250
142	Henry Washington	1728	336
205	John Elliott	1728	215
206	Same	1728	105

Book "D."

18	Wm. Brown	1731	105
71	James Thomas, Jr.	1731	24

Book "E."

11	John Piper	1737	37
16	Richard Sutton	1737	50
17	Ralph Faulkner	1737	2,592
91	Wm. Duff	1739	1,539
92	Capt. John Watts	1739	593
151	Samuel Davis	1740	59
283	Wm. Brown	1741	105
304	Original Brown	1741	43
322	Wm. Fryer	1741	61A.1R.10Per.
486	Augustine Washington	1742	566

Book "F."

79	Capt. Augustine Washington	1742	289
86	Andrew Monroe	1742	71A.36P.

161	John Baily and Stephen Baily.....1744	73½
204	John Bushrod 1744	723
206	Matthew and Peter Rust........1744	358
261	Capt. Willoughby Newton.......1746	15
265	John Butler 1746	40½
287	Thomas Butler 1747	67
297	Wm. Baley 1748	295
291	Capt. Jos. Strother 1748	94
296	Charles Ashton 1748	32A.1R.32P.
302	Richard Moxley 1748	58
309	Willoughby Newton 1749	6
311	Wm. Strother 1749	190
314	Gabriel Johnston 1749	184
327	Peter Rust 1749	343
328	Same 1749	33½
333	Colo. George Lee 1750	28
336	Capt. Willoughby Newton 1750	1,130
338	Capt. Willoughby Newton 1750	166
366	John Bailey 170–	28A.35Per.

Book "I."

27	Wm. Bernard 1757	78A.12Per.
29	Wm. Bayley 1757	295
82	Robert Eskridge 1762	51
108	Samuel White 1764	195
162	Francis Garner 1768	45A.12R.17Po.
163	Frances Garner 1768	62A.1R.1Po.
189	Thomas Washington 1771	69A.7Po.
192	Philip Smith 1771	60
330	Pemberton Claughton 1778	121

Book "T."

| 82 | Gabriel Johnson ....1788 | 226 |
| 118 | James Nevison ....1788 | 498 |

Book "W."

| 203 | Ransdell Pierce ....1793 | 16A.28Po. |
| 205 | Gerard McKinney ....1793 | 28A.3R.25Po. |

Book "Y."

| 242 | John Rose ....Blank date | 48 |

Abbington (Abington), 3, 5, 10, 14, 25
Adington, 96
Aitken, 50
Akers, 39
Alderson, 22, 24
Allday, 3, 5
Allen, 27
Allerton, 14, 16, 19, 25, 27, 31, 44, 59, 75, 91, 96, 97
Alexander, 92, 94
Allison, 11, 13
Allson, 49
Allworthy, 27
Anckram, 6
Andrews, 96
Anderson, 28, 37, 47, 90
Annadale, 82
Angier, 4
Anton, 76
Applegate, 37
Arbell, 3
Arnold, 55, 92
Ariss, 37, 61
Armistead, 48
Armsley, 2
Arrington, 19, 21, 22, 23, 100
Arrowsmith, 54
Asbury (Asberry), 17, 45, 50, 58, 70, 98
Ashton, 17, 21, 28, 32, 38, 45, 46, 48, 55, 61, 63, 67, 68, 72, 91, 93, 99, 100, 101, 102
Astin, 8
Attwell (Atwell), 5, 6, 15, 20, 21, 35, 36, 43, 57, 58, 68, 83, 85, 99, 100
Atwood, 19, 22
Awbrey, 23, 35, 40, 58, 100
Awbury, 28, 29, 37
Aylett, 38, 48

Bachellor, 98
Bagge, 21
Bagnall, 89
Bagwell, 42
Bailey (Bayley, Baley), 6, 9, 14, 19, 20, 22, 24, 26, 28, 35, 39, 41, 45, 48, 49, 51, 52, 55, 63, 70, 71, 73, 77, 80, 86, 102
Baker, 22, 26, 31, 51, 58, 62, 64, 65, 66, 97
Baldridge, 1, 2, 3, 4
Baldrop (Baltrop), 94, 95
Ball, 31, 33, 34, 42, 47, 50, 65, 66, 99
Balser, 56
Balthrop, 63, 64, 92
Bankhead, 55, 57, 68, 74
Bannister (Banister), 39, 63
Banwell, 33
Barber, 61
Barecroft, 72
Barker, 43, 70
Barnard, 26, 77
Barnes, 36, 53
Barnett (Barnet), 41, 50, 55, 80, 95
Bartlett, 84
Barton, 10
Baseley, 4, 94
Bashaw, 49
Batchellor, 28
Bateman, 25
Bayne (Bayn), 63, 69, 74, 78, 81
Baynes, 77
Baynham, 3
Baxter, 22, 24, 30, 50, 62
Beach, 89
Beale (Beall), 38, 44, 81, 95, 100

Beard, 11, 15, 17, 19, 21, 24, 45, 67, 92, 94, 97, 100
Beckwith, 23, 39
Bell, 2, 5, 29, 51, 68
Bellfield, 54
Bennett, 1, 9, 15, 26, 37, 51, 57, 59, 66, 72, 75, 83, 84, 90, 99
Benum, 92
Beord, 16
Berbard, 39
Berkeley (Berkely), 64, 67, 70, 85, 86
Bernard, 32, 39, 57, 59, 65, 75, 76, 89, 102
Berry, 12
Berryman (Berriman, Buryman) 14, 21, 29, 37, 44, 55, 64, 66, 71, 78, 95, 98, 100
Beverley, 50
Biddle, 2, 94
Billings, 70
Bincks (Binks), 37, 45, 61
Birkett, 76
Bittey, 54
Blackburn, 42
Blackmore, 49
Blagdon, 14
Blagg (Blag), 7, 24, 34, 55, 94
Blanchflower, 12, 13, 20
Blundell, 17, 22, 39, 42, 72
Boocock, 95
Bolthrop, 58
Bonam (Bonum), 15, 22, 26, 34, 35, 39, 51, 94
Boor, 89
Booth, 12, 14, 19, 44, 63
Borrer (Borer), 33, 55
Booze, 93
Botham, 90
Bott, 69
Boush, 24
Bowcock, 42, 47, 57, 73
Bowling, 37
Boyce, 1
Boyleston, 19
Bragg, 62
Branham, 27, 63
Brannan (Brannen), 15, 30
Breechin, 29, 31
Brett, 95
Brenan (Brenon), 45, 100
Brent, 1, 8, 66, 89, 90, 91, 92, 93, 94, 96, 97
Brewer, 54, 99, 100
Bricke (Brickey), 34, 81
Bridger, 96
Bridges (Briges), 4, 12, 14, 62, 67, 69
Briggs, 74
Brinham, 101
Brinnon, 80, 86
Brion, 71
Briscoe (Brisco), 27, 36, 83
Broags, 35
Brock, 42
Broadhurst (Brodhurst), 1, 6, 91
Brooks (Brookes), 3, 92
Brooking, 61
Brown (Browne), 5, 10, 11, 15, 16, 17, 19, 21, 30, 32, 33, 36, 37, 39, 44, 48, 49, 50, 58, 59, 60, 62, 64, 67, 68, 69, 70, 72, 75, 82, 85, 89, 91, 92, 94, 95, 97, 98, 99, 101
Browning, 35
Bruce, 47
Bruceton, 93
Bryant, 25

Buckley, 12, 13, 39
Buckner, 74, 82
Buckocks, 92
Bulger, 41, 70, 78
Burch, 39
Burns (Burn, Burne), 32, 34, 71
Burshaw, 73
Burwell, 3
Bush, 46
Bushrod, 28, 31, 44, 56, 60, 91, 92, 99, 102
Butler (Buttler), 3, 6, 8, 9, 12, 17, 18, 19, 20, 21, 22, 26, 28, 29, 30, 31, 36, 37, 39, 40, 47, 48, 52, 54, 55, 57, 58, 59, 60, 64, 67, 72, 73, 74, 75, 79, 83, 84, 86, 92, 93, 94, 95, 99, 100, 101, 102
Byard, 29, 99

Cadeen, 61
Callis (Calles), 52, 59, 61, 68, 75
Cahoe, 21
Campbell, 14
Campian, 5
Canada, 14
Cannady (Cannaday), 39, 77
Cardwell, 23
Carey (Cary), 3, 89, 90
Carmichael, 76
Carnhill, 97
Carpenter, 37, 71, 79, 99
Carr, 14, 15, 30, 35, 46
Carrier, 9
Carroll, 22
Carter, 17, 28, 29, 31, 46, 74, 79, 82, 99, 101
Cash, 18
Cavender, 70
Chalker, 33
Chambers, 47
Chancellor, 16, 33, 41, 61
Chandler, 28, 60, 79
Chanlor, 34, 37, 100
Chapman, 6, 23, 43
Charles, 21
Chilton, 18, 24, 25, 34, 41, 42, 65, 71, 85, 86, 99, 100
Christopher, 15
Chubb, 13
Churnell, 9
Clarke (Clark), 9, 11, 23, 28, 84
Claughton, 48, 102
Clay, 4, 94
Clayton, 19
Claytor (Clator, Claiter), 27, 29, 38, 49, 56, 58, 77, 96
Clemens, 21
Clements, 13
Clington, 52
Cochren, 19
Cock, 82
Cockerill, 14, 36, 52
Cockrell, 55
Codsford, 89, 90
Coe, 92
Coggin, 20
Coghill, 68
Cohoren, 18
Cole (Coale), 3, 18, 19, 90, 98
Coleman, 4, 12, 30, 41, 51, 95
Collier, 23
Collin, 21
Collins, 5, 23, 29, 31, 71, 86
Collinsworth (Collingsworth), 6, 41, 53, 70, 76, 79, 83, 96
Colson, 23

Conditt, 40
Conelly, 76
Coneland, 15
Conniers, 23, 59, 75
Connoly, 77
Conner, 27
Cooper, 32, 37, 41, 44
Cope, 47
Corbin, 38, 50, 53, 60
Cossum, 3, 91, 95
Couch, 23
Court, 92
Courtney, 42, 58, 61, 72, 79
Courtwell, 27, 33
Coward, 66
Cox, 12, 20, 39, 48, 50, 53, 56, 60, 61, 63, 66, 68, 72, 84, 85, 99
Coy, 94
Crabb, 20, 25, 28, 43, 53, 72, 77, 81
Craddock (Cradock), 19, 20, 30, 95
Craddunck, 12
Craighill, 60
Crawford, 53
Creed, 40, 49
Crenshaw, 80
Creswick, 43
Critcher, 51
Croswell, 98
Cross, 13, 16
Croutchman, 24
Crumnil, 53
Crutcher, 67
Cullum, 10
Cupingheiffer, 69
Curtis, 21, 43, 91
Cutler, 20

Dab, 30
Dade, 8
Damavorell, 30
Daneley, 49
Dangerfield, 72
Danielson, 55
Danks, 17
Dark, 16
Davenport, 16, 72, 82
Davies, 23
Davis, 12, 19, 20, 28, 31, 46, 51, 52, 63, 64, 65, 70, 72, 97, 100, 101
Day, 1
Deane, 57, 86
Deatterley, 57
Degges, 71
Delozier, 65, 72
Delria, 10
Demenet, 14
Demovel, 48
Deshman, 44
Dickinson, 42
Dickson, 45
Dishman, 36, 59, 69, 71, 75
Dios, 93
Dodd, 48, 63, 73, 81
Dodman, 91
Dodson, 5, 89, 91
Dolman, 78
Douglass, 64
Dowling, 32, 57
Downing, 24, 84
Downton, 21
Doyle, 2
Dozer, 71
Dozier, 40, 54, 76, 82, 83, 86
Drake, 78, 79, 82, 84
Draper, 1
Drayton, 91, 93

Driskall, 28
Drummond, 91
Duckworth, 4
Duckiminia, 99
Duddlestone, 21
Dudley, 14, 31
Duff, 101
Dulin, 60
Dulstone, 8
Dunahaw, 98
Dunbar, 62
Duncan (Dunkan), 19, 26, 50, 98
Dunkin (Dunken), 5, 10, 35, 51, 59, 75, 95
Dunn, 29
Duren, 43
During, 32
Durwin, 44
Duthrie, 67
Dutton, 3
Dyar, 94
Dye, 2

Eales, 30
Earl, 49
Earls, 46
Eastaff, 3
Eaton, 27
Eattle, 22
Edrington, 71, 76, 85
Edwards, 19, 56, 72, 74, 85, 86, 97
Elinore, 78
Elliott, 18, 19, 22, 25, 34, 45, 52, 53, 58, 59, 75, 101
Ellis, 91
Elston, 31
English, 5, 6, 13, 34
Erwin, 23
Eskridge, 7, 14, 15, 16, 25, 26, 29, 32, 34, 37, 41, 44, 48, 98, 99, 101, 102
Esther, 39
Ethell (Ethel), 11, 24, 51
Eustace, 59, 75
Evans, 6, 91

Fairfax, 62
Fauntleroy, 28, 44
Faulkner, 101
Feagin, 72
Fenn, 23
Field (Fields), 15, 28, 30, 39, 58, 98
Fielder, 49
Finch, 25, 41, 46, 47, 55, 65
Fisher, 50, 96
FitzGarrett, 98
Fitzhugh, 22, 32, 38, 80, 81, 97
Fleming, 45, 48, 66
Fletcher, 20
Flewelling, 9
Fling, 55
Flint, 17
Flood, 73
Follings, 14
Foot, 64
Footman, 23, 44, 48, 90
Ford, 17, 28, 50
Forster, 96
Foster, 15
Fowke, 3, 89, 93, 95
Fox, 67
Foxhall, 9, 19, 95
Frank (Franke), 32, 35, 55, 71, 96
Franklin (Frankline), 52, 53, 55, 68, 79, 83, 96
Freeke, 93
Freeld, 44

Freshwater, 81
Frissell, 93
Frizzar, 89
Froud, 30
Fryer (Fryar), 32, 36, 70, 97, 101
Furgeson, 57
Furlong, 24

Gammon, 29
Gannack, 31
Gardner (Gardener), 98, 99
Garland, 7, 15, 20, 40, 41, 43, 48, 65, 85, 96
Garner, 15, 20, 23, 26, 41, 44, 49, 51, 58, 61, 68, 72, 81, 99, 100, 102
Garrard, 50, 53, 62, 67, 74, 75
Gathagin, 55
George, 38
Gerrard (Gerard), 1, 2, 11, 19, 20, 23, 24, 30, 59, 100
Gerviss, 39
Gibbs, 47
Gibson, 28
Gilbert, 26, 65, 74, 80, 82, 83
Gilpin, 32
Glasco, 33
Gobbs, 43
Goff, 29, 52, 66
Golding, 31
Golorthum, 39
Gooch, 89
Good, 13
Goodwin, 91
Gordon, 10, 76, 80
Gore, 28
Gough, 24, 33
Gower, 14, 22
Grace, 49, 50, 68
Graham, 14, 15, 24
Grant, 55
Granger, 95
Grase, 44
Grasty, 99
Graves, 90
Green, 13, 17, 37, 57, 79, 82, 93, 94
Greenwood, 49
Greg (Grigg), 94, 95
Grey (Gray), 4, 18, 22, 40, 47, 55, 93, 100, 101
Griffen (Griffin), 24, 40, 92
Griggs, 79
Grigsby, 64, 78
Grimstead (Grimestead), 19
Grinning, 35
Groves, 18
Gullock (Gulluck), 12, 97
Guiness, 51

Haborn, 55
Hackney, 49
Halcom, 51
Hales, 36, 57
Haley (Hailey or Haelly), 6, 14, 74, 94
Hall, 53, 62, 70, 84
Halliday, 37, 54
Hallowes (Hallows), 1, 92
Ham, 19
Hambleton, 35
Hammock, 17, 97, 98
Hancock, 6, 18
Handley, 29
Hardage, 32
Hardich (Hardidge), 2, 8, 38, 52, 93
Hardwich, 35

Hardwick, 9, 12, 17, 20, 27, 38, 40, 43, 51, 97
Hardwitch, 101
Hardy, 23
Hargis, 37
Harness, 40
Harper, 17, 19, 70, 81, 86
Harris, 10, 12, 33, 91, 92, 94, 97
Harrison, 21, 26, 30, 33, 37, 40, 43, 46, 52, 54, 55, 58, 60, 65, 67, 70, 71, 74, 77, 80, 89, 90, 97
Hart, 96
Hartley, 36, 48, 97
Harvey, 33, 85, 97
Haselrigg (Haselrig), 21, 40
Hath, 46
Haven, 25
Hawkins, 14, 89
Hawley, 25, 95
Hayden (Haydon), 5, 34
Hays (Hayes), 41, 48
Hayward, 93
Hazelrigg, 50, 56
Heabord (Heaberd), 91, 92, 93, 94
Heabron, 76
Headley, 21, 25, 46, 72
Heale, 46
Hearn, 11
Hemmings, 27
Hennings, 17
Henman, 15
Henmons, 21
Henry, 38, 67
Herley, 50
Herney, 33
Herra, 25
Hewes, 11
Hewgate, 98
Hicking, 24
Hicks, 6
Higden (Higdon), 3, 14, 27, 29, 33, 44, 51, 69
Higgenson (Higginson), 89, 100
Higgins, 14, 18, 19, 29
Hillier, 1
Hilton, 64, 65, 67, 74
Hindmer, 20
Hines, 7, 23
Hinson, 77
Hipkins, 80
Hoare (Hore), 19, 20, 34, 64, 99
Hobson, 23, 46
Hoburd, 30
Hodgson, 66
Hogg, 12, 17
Holladay (Holliday), 39, 42
Hollam, 35
Holland, 52, 62, 70, 80
Holloway, 82
Hopkins, 17
Hopwood, 33
Hord, 10, 33, 60
Hornbuckle (Hornebuckle), 17, 99
Hornby, 44
Horrell, 15, 43
Horton, 7, 12, 63, 93, 94, 95
Houell, 24
Howard, 23, 25
Howell, 15, 43
Hubard (Hubbard or Hubord), 7, 89, 90
Hudson, 6, 12, 16, 18, 28, 42, 98
Hull, 16, 61
Humes, 83
Humphreys (Humphries), 25, 92
Hungerford, 86

Hunter, 74
Hurley, 18, 23, 66
Hutcheson, 56, 67, 92
Hutchinson, 35
Hutson, 39
Hutt, 1, 4, 20, 45, 47, 50, 68, 70, 77, 94, 99

Igdon, 16
Iglis, 69
Inman, 3
Ireland, 4
Isham, 2

Jackson, 32, 48, 51, 54, 55, 56, 58, 59, 66, 67, 68, 75, 77, 79
Jadwin, 5, 9
James, 42, 49, 58, 101
Jarvis, 17, 21, 48
Jarnew, 93
Jeffreys (Jeffries), 32, 40, 41, 64, 66, 72, 78
Jenkins, 25, 30, 34, 40, 47, 55, 62, 70, 76
Jennings, 20, 28, 36, 37
Jett, 39, 40, 44, 56, 57, 61, 66, 72, 76, 82, 83, 84, 85, 86
Jewell, 31, 44
Joanes, 91
Johnson, 14, 19, 23, 61, 77, 89
Johnston (Johnstone), 4, 11, 66, 102
Joncel, 56
Jones, 2, 3, 6, 7, 12, 14, 15, 20, 21, 25, 27, 36, 55, 72, 73, 74, 93, 98
Jordan, 7, 18, 47, 54, 71
Journew, 5
Joyce, 20

Keating, 37
Keene, 36
Keesee, 31
Kelley (Kelly), 28, 32, 83
Kelsick, 77, 78
Kemp, 86
Kendall, 42, 52, 55
Kenner (Kennar), 28, 30, 41, 48, 59, 66, 75
Kersey, 64
Kill, 52
Kimball, 10
King, 17, 26, 34, 36
Kirk (Kirke), 54, 65, 94, 95, 97
Kirkland, 93
Kirkham, 81
Kitchen, 79
Kitching, 30
Knight, 12
Knighton, 35
Knoble, 16
Koherin, 98

Lacy, 81
Lafon, 68
Laham, 14
Lambee, 14
Lambert, 23, 29, 50, 76
Lambkin, 30, 35, 43, 48, 50, 52, 54, 60, 62, 63, 70, 81
Lampkin, 4
Lancelott, 3, 4, 17, 19
Landman, 6
Lane, 28, 51, 60, 66, 81, 85, 86
Langford, 17
Lankford, 23
Lansdowne, 4
Latham (Lathom), 99
Latharam, 32

Lawrence, 69
Lawson, 66, 76, 77
Laycock, 23
Lear, 90
Lee, 14, 15, 22, 23, 25, 32, 34, 38, 46, 50, 53, 59, 60, 62, 63, 65, 66, 75, 83, 85, 86, 91, 95, 99, 100, 102
Leftwich, 17, 74
Legg, 16
Lenham, 13
Letts, 4
Lewis, 10, 26, 28, 30, 40, 41, 53, 63, 70, 74, 81, 90, 91, 94
Lindsey, 1
Linton, 40
Longworth, 29, 32, 36, 54, 71
Lord, 4, 94, 96
Loudoun, 1
Lovell, 11, 16, 22, 23, 24, 28, 33, 36, 40, 43, 54, 76, 95
Lowe, 61, 77
Loyd, 94
Lucas, 15, 17, 23
Luck, 48
Ludwell, 95
Luke, 22
Lund, 2
Luttrell, 30, 68
Lyn, 15
Lynsey, 31

McAulay, 58
McBoyd, 27, 50
McClanahan, 45, 69, 71
McCarney, 43
McCarty (McCarthy), 15, 28, 29, 32, 38, 40, 44, 48, 82, 98, 101
McClave, 51
McCulloch (McCullock), 42, 49
McFarlane, 55, 56
McFarlans, 50
McKenna (McKenne), 39, 56
McKenney (McKenny), 43, 48, 53, 57, 72, 78, 79, 85
McKettrick, 77
McKinney, 86, 102
McLarran, 44
Macclanacon, 26
Macgill, 38
Macormack, 52
Maddison, 2, 9
Maders, 19
Maiders, 11
Manley, 24
Manner, 18
Manning, 18, 32
Mansell, 89
Maphe, 2, 3
Marcy (Marcey), 15, 32
Markham, 16, 20, 97, 98, 99
Marloe, 26
Marmaduke, 6, 39, 62, 78, 86
Marrean, 23
Marrice, 97
Marshall, 16, 54, 71, 73, 85
Marson, 14, 20, 96
Marteaw, 89
Martin (Martyn), 5, 16, 29, 33, 36, 39, 49, 77, 85, 90, 98
Mason, 28, 33
Massey (Massie), 11, 24, 26, 28, 56, 65, 73, 81
Matrom, 89, 93
Mauley, 99
Maunder, 4, 93
Mazengo, 19

Meacham, 36
Medford, 26
Meeks, 78
Meldrum, 47
Melvin, 37
Meriwether (Merywether), 28, 44, 90
Merker, 30
Merman, 41
Merrick, 98
Middleton, 7, 12, 15, 17, 37, 39, 48, 55, 58, 60, 61, 64, 68, 69, 70, 72, 81, 83, 84, 85, 94
Miles, 90
Miller, 10, 57
Mills, 17
Minor, 12, 29, 30, 32, 34, 41, 42, 45, 48, 51, 53, 99, 100
Mockridge, 49
Modiset, 73
Monroe, 38, 42, 43, 45, 52, 55, 59, 62, 68, 69, 70, 74, 75, 78, 79, 80, 85, 86, 101
Moon (Moone), 25, 89
Moore (More), 20, 41, 43, 44, 47, 48, 52, 63, 69, 73, 86
Morgan, 4, 16, 69, 81, 85
Morphew, 36
Morris, 21, 29, 33, 35, 44, 83
Morrison, 40
Morse, 76
Morton, 28, 38, 65, 83, 84
Moss, 18, 36
Mottershead (Mothershead), 27, 38, 46, 49, 52, 58, 62, 63, 69, 77, 93
Mouerly, 97
Mountjoy, 96
Moxle, 18
Moxley, 21, 41, 48, 60, 63, 66, 69, 71, 74, 78, 82, 102
Muckleroy, 27
Mullins, 37, 61, 78
Munn, 2
Munroe, 7, 13, 16, 18, 22, 33, 58, 59, 75, 97
Murphy, 22, 30, 47
Muse, 29, 30, 34, 38, 40, 41, 42, 43, 44, 53, 54, 58, 59, 60, 65, 68, 70, 75, 76, 77, 78, 79, 82, 84, 85, 98, 99
Mussett, 63
Mustin, 22

Naillor, 56
Nash, 35, 51, 62, 70, 72, 78, 79
Naughty, 59, 62, 67, 75
Neale, 21, 42, 43, 44, 46, 56, 59, 69, 71, 75, 76, 82, 97
Nelson, 64, 85, 86
Netherton, 25
Nevison, 102
Newberry, 4
Newell, 12
Newgent, 26
Newmarch, 62
Newstubbs, 15
Newman, 38
Newton, 7, 8, 14, 19, 20, 23, 31, 36, 41, 48, 51, 56, 66, 67, 77, 101, 102
Nicholson, 33
Nicholas, 11
Nicholls, 25, 54, 97
Nobell, 16
Norman, 91
Notts, 11
Nowel, 57

INDEX

Nowles, 64
Nutt, 47
Nurse, 95

Occany, 25, 34
Offile, 19
Olathman, 5
Oliff, 50
Omohundro, 10, 35, 65, 82, 83, 97
Oneal, 31
Orr, 61
Orchard, 15
Osborne, 15
Overed, 91
Overall (Overhall), 20, 100
Overett, 94
Owen, 5, 26, 27

Packett, 52, 76, 78
Padgett, 51
Paine (Payne), 8, 14, 32, 42
Palmer, 27, 92, 95
Parker, 6, 73, 82, 84, 86, 89
Parsley, 73
Parsons, 25, 70
Partington, 2
Partridge, 35, 52, 60, 69
Pary, 44
Pate, 92
Paten, 39
Patton, 89
Payne, 5, 9, 11, 44, 53, 67, 82, 83, 96
Peach (Peack), 33
Peachey, 32
Peal, 95
Pears (Pearce), 10, 11, 12, 94
Pearse, 45
Pease, 22
Peck, 55
Pennell, 10, 11
Pepper, 11, 12
Perkins, 2, 13
Perry (Perrie), 44, 60, 94
Pettigrew, 93
Pettit, 60, 72
Pettus, 91
Peyton (Payton), 2, 4, 38, 48, 79, 84, 90, 91, 93
Phelps, 5
Phillips (Philips), 15, 90, 91, 98
Phillpot, 93, 95
Pickerill, 15
Pickett, 46
Pierce, 14, 23, 32, 40, 59, 73, 75, 76, 95, 96, 102
Piecroft, 6
Pinckard, 71
Piper, 17, 32, 59, 66, 73, 75, 95, 101
Plunkett, 35
Poindexter, 31
Pope, 1, 2, 5, 8, 10, 11, 14, 17, 18, 22, 24, 27, 28, 29, 30, 32, 40, 44, 46, 49, 51 54, 57, 60, 73, 77, 80, 89, 90, 91, 92, 93, 98, 100
Popham, 44, 100
Porten, 21, 24
Porter, 57, 65, 67, 72, 76, 77, 78, 98, 100
Potter, 27
Powell, 18, 21
Power, 28
Pownall, 46
Pratt, 22, 25, 61, 100
Prescott, 3
Price, 18, 26, 28, 47, 54, 56, 58, 60, 76
Pridham, 54

Pritchett, 30, 39, 63, 66
Purslee, 34
Purvis, 20
Pye, 15

Quigley, 95
Quill, 44
Quisenberry (Quesenbury), 12, 26, 30, 38, 39, 46, 49, 52, 56, 63, 67, 73, 81
Quoanes, 4

Raffedy, 43
Rallings (Rallins), 45, 52, 55, 56
Ramery, 30
Randall, 65, 79
Randolph, 16
Ransdell, 23, 32, 35, 41, 44, 45, 59, 65, 73, 75, 82, 98
Rawlings, 24
Read (Reed, Reid, Reade), 7, 12, 13, 31, 50, 67, 68, 70, 91, 94, 97, 99
Reamy, 97
Redman, 11, 16, 23, 28, 61, 76, 77, 78, 83
Rele, 31
Remy, 36, 43, 46
Render, 41
Reynes, 4
Reynolds, 48, 65
Rhodes, 51
Ribets, 60
Rice, 7, 17, 32, 39, 48, 59, 71, 75, 80, 85, 86, 96
Richards, 85
Richardson, 49
Rigg, 71
Riley, 32
Roach, 90, 91
Roberson, 58
Roberts, 14
Robertson, 25
Robins, 6, 15, 19, 100
Robinson, 17, 29, 32, 33, 38, 43, 62, 70, 72, 77, 79, 85, 89
Robottom, 25
Rochester, 35, 53, 58, 71, 85, 86
Roe, 10, 14, 18, 24, 58, 96
Rogers, 10, 49, 93
Rollins, 26
Rose, 61, 102
Rosier, 90, 92
Roussau, 53
Rouzee, 58
Rowbotham, 44
Rowe, 67
Rowland, 30, 38
Rowsey, 14
Rozier, 1, 2, 8, 12, 14, 16, 17
Ruch, 18
Rush, 4, 18, 19, 36, 74, 98
Russell, 36, 53, 65, 100
Rust, 7, 13, 26, 30, 36, 37, 38, 41, 46, 49, 50, 53, 54, 55, 56, 60, 62, 69, 74, 79, 80, 81, 84, 102
Rutherford, 69

Sanford, 12, 18, 31, 34, 38, 39, 40, 42 43, 44, 46, 51, 53, 54, 57, 60, 62, 66, 67, 68, 77, 78, 80, 81, 82, 84, 85, 86, 96, 98
Salter, 4
Sanders, 29, 34, 36, 43, 100
Sandford, 56
Sandy, 62

Saunders, 43
Saxton, 3, 18
Scott, 13, 14, 16, 50, 74, 77, 98
Scutt, 76
Sears, 66
Searle (Searles), 91, 95
Seaton, 90
Self (Selfe), 25, 40, 62, 77, 92, 98, 99, 100
Sebastin, 26
Settle, 56, 61
Shadrack, 59, 75
Sharp (Sharpe), 18, 42, 45
Shaw, 14, 19, 25, 41, 46
Sheadrick, 24
Shearman, 61
Shephard (Shepherd), 20, 29
Sheppard, 15
Sherman, 32
Shinroe, 97
Shoats, 83
Shore, 3, 6, 91
Shortridge, 26
Shropshire, 47, 99
Silvey, 39
Simmons, 11, 19
Simpson, 86
Sisson, 2, 11
Slye, 1
Smith, 3, 6, 7, 12, 14, 17, 21, 22, 23, 24, 27, 29, 33, 38, 40, 41, 45, 46, 47, 50, 52, 53, 54, 61, 62, 63, 66, 67, 70, 71, 72, 74, 76, 77, 78, 79, 81, 82, 83, 85, 86, 90, 94, 96, 98, 99, 100, 102
Smoot, 17
Smooth, 98
Solley, 8
Sorn, 50
Sorrell, 22, 23, 25, 26, 28, 31, 34, 61, 80, 83, 99, 100
South, 23, 29, 60, 66
Spark, 67
Sparrow, 26, 30
Speed, 24
Speke, 1, 2, 4
Spellman, 27, 57
Spence, 1, 6, 7, 9, 16, 18, 23, 26, 34, 35, 45, 56, 80, 86, 91, 95, 98, 101
Spencer, 5, 6, 18, 29, 95, 96
Spenson, 94
Spiller, 29
Spilman (Spillman), 35, 60, 65
Spurling, 33, 34
Stands, 3
Stapleton, 50
Starks, 77
Starr, 14
Steel (Steele), 31, 42, 46, 47, 52, 78, 83, 101
Stephens, 19, 32, 33, 45, 71, 90
Steptoe, 59, 75, 78
Stereman, 94
Steward, 73, 103
Stewart, 17
Stone, 26, 31, 41, 42, 57, 69, 80
Stonehouse, 47
Stopper, 6
Storke, 28, 32, 57, 72
Streater, 90
Strother, 42, 47, 57, 63, 76, 102
Strowder, 91
Struder, 92
Stowers, 51, 69
Stuart, 43, 101
Sturman, 5, 6, 7, 18, 25, 31, 34, 38, 41, 43, 45, 65, 73, 84, 93, 94, 100, 101

Suggett, 56
Sullivan, 13
Summers, 37, 51
Summerville, 25
Sutherland, 29
Sutton, 50, 52, 56, 80, 96, 99, 101

Talbot (Talbott), 11, 32
Taliaferro, 64
Tancell, 21
Tankersley, 16
Tanner, 15, 18, 40, 96
Tasker, 7, 74
Taverner, 44
Tayloe, 32, 38, 46
Taylor, 10, 12, 14, 18, 19, 29, 32, 37, 38, 42, 49, 53, 56, 65, 71, 76, 97
Tebbs, 50, 51, 53, 64, 73
Templeman, 52, 54, 80, 84
Tew, 1
Thomas, 11, 16, 27, 28, 35, 44, 45, 47, 56, 67, 90, 101
Thompson (Thomson), 8, 23, 25, 54, 56, 57, 68, 97, 98
Thornbury, 15, 24
Thorne (Thorn), 10, 16, 80, 97
Thornton, 39, 54, 100
Thrasnall, 50
Tidwell, 62, 64, 82
Tillary, 14
Tilson, 14
Tingle, 62
Tilt, 92
Todd, 61
Tomlin, 40
Travers (Traverse), 14, 94
Triplett, 14, 64, 76, 85, 86
Trussell, 4
Tucker, 5, 29, 60, 98
Tupman, 74
Turberville, 31, 34, 38, 43, 46, 62, 85, 99
Turner, 27, 79, 82, 101
Turnbull, 78
Tunbridge, 10, 11
Tupper, 92
Tyler, 22, 43
Tynon, 44

Underwood, 18

Vanlendgen, 21
Vaughan, 2, 3, 27, 41
Vaulx, 9, 19, 21, 26, 30, 49, 55, 59, 75, 90
Vauly, 89, 90, 93
Veale (Veel), 6, 27
Vigar (Vigor), 66, 69
Vincent, 4, 13, 92, 93
Vivion, 61

Waddey, 30, 34, 40
Wading, 92
Walker, 4, 14, 15, 22, 23, 26, 35, 37, 39, 40, 43, 53, 61, 65, 66, 69, 70, 73
Wall, 89
Walls, 25
Walton, 89
Ward, 27, 36, 46
Warden, 73
Ware, 16, 45
Warman, 94
Washington, 2, 5, 8, 16, 20, 21, 30, 31, 33, 39, 45, 48, 50, 57, 59, 60, 62, 65, 72, 75, 79, 81, 82, 86, 92, 96, 97, 101, 102

Waters, 24, 26
Watson, 30, 41, 93
Wattey, 21
Watts, 3, 5, 6, 13, 16, 21, 22, 24, 25, 34, 35, 37, 38, 42, 45, 55, 100, 101
Wauhopes, 36
Weading (Weeding), 92, 94
Weaver, 65, 69, 77, 78, 81
Webb, 3, 5, 11, 21, 95
Webster, 14, 15
Weedon, 3, 7, 16, 18, 19, 40, 45, 47, 55, 58, 64, 67, 71, 95, 96, 97
Weeks (Weekes), 24, 25, 34, 47, 49, 52, 77, 78
Welch, 25, 49, 56
Wells, 91
Wellington, 17, 43
West, 10, 44
Westcomb, 17, 23
Wharton, 17, 98
Wheeler, 24, 28, 63, 96, 100
Whetstone, 94
Whiston, 5
White, 11, 13, 36, 49, 53, 62, 64, 65, 67, 92, 93, 95, 97, 102
Whitehouse, 100
Whiting, 28, 56, 58, 59, 75
Wickers, 16
Wickliffe, 11, 13
Wickoff, 9
Wigginton, 23, 27, 31, 39, 50
Wigley, 76

Wild, 93
Wilkerson, 55, 58, 64
Wilkinson, 60
Williams, 11, 12, 14, 21, 26, 35, 39, 40, 42, 46, 51, 60, 61, 73, 91, 96, 97, 100
Williamson, 28
Willis, 21, 95
Wilsford, 1, 5, 16, 90, 93
Wilson (Willson), 5, 21, 28, 30, 54, 55
Winder, 28
Windsor, 77
Windzor, 11
Withers, 90, 91, 95
Woffendall, 95
Wood, 21, 51, 90, 93
Woddier, 28
Woodlock, 15
Woodward, 29
Worden, 24
Wormoth, 43
Woring, 37
Wright, 21, 22, 23, 39, 46, 50, 56, 58, 63, 66, 72, 81, 84, 91, 96, 98, 99
Wroe, 33, 37, 52, 74, 76, 81
Wyatt, 21, 29

Yeatman, 85
Yellop, 47
Yoe, 89
Youell (Youel, Yowell), 6, 35, 48, 95
Young, 41, 47, 84, 92